WHERE
HOPE
GROWS
FREE

To my dear friend Ramani: May you come to realize that God cultivates your heart as carefully as you tend to the people and plants in your life.

Hello!

Grab your Bible and prepare to take a nature walk through God's Word. Visit the accounts of the world's very first garden, the tree where our Savior died, and the Tree of Life that awaits each of us who have committed our lives to Christ. Use the lessons to nourish your spiritual roots and bear good fruit to bless those in your life.

This beautiful world we live in tells the incredible life-changing story of our God and His love for each one of us. There are many ways to study the Bible—the living, breathing Word of God, and one way is through nature itself. The Bible tells us:

> *For His invisible attributes, namely, His eternal power and divine nature, have been clearly perceived, ever since the creation of the world, in the things that have been made. So they are without excuse.* –Romans 1:20

May this study plant a seed in your heart that will grow into a thriving tree, planted by streams of living water.

Lessons to Strengthen Spiritual Roots

The World's First Garden

Gardeners and farmers know how much care goes into preparing, planting, and maintaining healthy plants and trees. God gave that same thoughtful care to the world's first garden when He created the earth.

On day one of creation, God draws a boundary between light and dark—providing the light plants need to grow and the dark so they will not scorch. On day two of creation, dry ground with rich soil is made, perfectly suited for the vegetation that is to come. At the sound of God's voice on day three, the land bursts forth with greenery. Plants, grass, flowers and trees fill the earth. Our amazing God notices and cares for each little lily of the field (Matthew 6:28-29). On day four, God provides the sun that fuels the process of photosynthesis for plants—how they receive nutrients. Day five brings birds which play a role in spreading seeds. On day six, humans and the rest of the animals are masterfully created, including pollinators like bees and butterflies. Each plant and each animal is meticulously created to work in harmony in the world that our God lovingly set into motion.

It seems God, with His incredible eye for beauty, has a special place in His heart for plants and trees. After creating plants and trees, God says it is "very good." Notice that most days of creation are noted as "good" but plants and trees are "very good." When God draws emphasis to something, we should take note! From this point on in the Bible, we see plants and trees are part of every major account in the history of God's love and plan for us.

The last day of creation (day 6), God creates people and places them in a carefully planted garden called the Garden of Eden. Each day of creation builds upon the last and perfectly provides everything needed for this garden: light, soil, the sun, pollinators, and caretakers. Likewise, the garden is perfectly suited for everything animals and humans need to thrive. At the center of this garden is a beautiful tree called the Tree of Life that someday, God's children will see again!

The world's first garden is created to serve many purposes. It is a place to live, a place where nourishment can be found, and a place to enjoy. It is where humans can walk alongside God in the cool of the day (Genesis 3:8). Can you imagine walking in this garden with God? Humans were first created to live amongst the plants and trees, and it is interesting that science is just now catching up with the idea of how important being in nature is to human health and well-being.

In *Forest Bathing: How Trees Can Help You Find Health and Happiness*, Dr. Li notes inhabitants of Western countries are spending an increasing amount of time indoors to the detriment of physical and mental health. Currently, it is reported that Americans spend 93% of their time indoors. One-fourth of Americans spend their *entire* day indoors. That means we spend less than half a day outdoors a week. Being inside, we are unable to access the life-giving and enhancing power of nature that God created. Indoor time brings about its own hazards. Indoor air is more polluted than outdoor air, causing increased health risks. In addition, those indoors tend to be less physically active than their peers who spend more time outside. While indoors, Americans spend close to 11 hours on a screen consuming media. Screen time increases stress, anxiety, insomnia, depression, isolation, and has even been linked to PTSD type symptoms.[1]

Dr. Li found that a very small shift in choices brought about a drastic change in health and wellness. Spending just two hours outside in nature helps reduce blood pressure, lower stress, improve heart health, lower blood sugar levels, improve focus, boost creativity, lessen depression, increase energy, improve sleep, raise your protection against cancer, and boost your immune system. The outdoors offers more benefits than most medications can boast.[1]

In addition to physical health benefits, there are mental health benefits from being outdoors. A study in the UK found that people who live near trees are happier and those who live near trees live longer.[2] Science is now pointing to the truth that God authored from the very beginning—the natural world is perfectly suited for humans to thrive in. Not only are our physical health and mental health enhanced by being outdoors, but research also acknowledges that our spiritual health is positively impacted by time in nature! A Michigan State University study found that children who spent at least 10 hours outdoors a week reported a greater sense of peacefulness and were more likely to believe in a higher power.[3] What a tremendous gift we can offer ourselves and those around us by simply spending more time in God's wonderful creation.

However, as perfect as this first garden is and how amazing it is to walk with God, it is not enough to satisfy the world's first couple. The woman Eve is approached by a serpent who is known as the craftiest creature on earth. The serpent challenges the only rule God had instituted—not to eat from the Tree of Knowledge of Good and Evil. God warned the couple that eating of the tree would bring death and forbid them from eating from it. The serpent challenges the words of God and plants a seed of doubt in the mind of the woman by telling her she would not die, but become more like God. This seed of doubting God is cultivated in her mind as she sees the fruit appears pleasing and that power of knowledge is just as desirable. She makes the choice to eat it and offers some to Adam who also eats the fruit.

In the moment it takes to pluck a piece of fruit off a tree and eat it, Adam and Eve's entire existence and the existence of the rest of the human race is forever changed. Sin enters the world and harshly separates humans from their Maker. Adam and Eve feel shame for the first time and hide. God asks them what they have done. Adam a Eve's eyes are opened to evil and they realize they are naked. Despite their poor choices, God continues to provide. We see here the world's first sacrifice for sin—an animal has to die in order for the couple to be clothed with its skin. This idea of needing a sacrifice for sin is a key concept we will see throughout the Bible, and ultimately in the life and death of Jesus Christ. Though life is forever changed and Adam and Eve are banned from the garden, we see God still cares for and provides for His precious creation.

Prayer

Lord, maker of heaven and earth, the one who designed beautiful flowers and such an amazing variety of tasty and healthy fruit trees, thank You. Thank You for providing what we need not only to survive, but to thrive.

As we learn more about this garden and Your ultimate plan for each one of us, please plant Your seed of truth in our hearts. Allow our hearts to be fertile ground, ready for new growth to spring forth. And let Your truth in our hearts grow deep roots and bear good fruit for we long to walk and talk with you under the shade of the trees, just we were created to do.

In Jesus' most holy name,
Amen (comes from the Hebrew word meaning "so be it")

1. Read Genesis 1–3. What do you find interesting or notable in this account?

2. Why does God plant trees in the garden? What are the special trees? (Genesis 2:8-9)

3. How is the fruit from the forbidden tree described? (Genesis 3:6)

4. Before sin, how would you have described Adam and Eve's relationship with God?

_____

_____

5. What changes after Adam and Eve decided to eat the fruit? (Genesis 3:22)

_____

_____

6. Why is the Tree of Life guarded after sin entered the world? (Genesis 3:22-23)

_____

_____

7. What can we learn about God from this account?

_____

_____

_____

A Single Olive Branch

In the generations following Adam and Eve, the inhabitants of the earth turn further and further away from God and follow their own desires and wicked intentions. The earth is full of violence. Noah alone is found to be following God. He is described as blameless in his generation and as a man that walks with God (Genesis 6:8).

This blatant disregard for God and mankind's propensity for violence leads to a significant consequence—a worldwide flood. God directs Noah to build an ark. The ark, built in a desert region nowhere near the sea, must have been quite the sight. Yet Noah does not question God; and his faith and obedience results in Noah, his family, and every type of animal to be spared from the flood that covers the entire earth and wipes out every living thing.

For 40 long days, relentless rain beats against the ark. The surface of the earth suffers a massive flood, drowning everything and everyone that isn't on the ark. What a terrifying time this must have been for the people who ignored God's warning and found themselves outside the boat when the rain began beating down. Despite the raging waters and world-wide devastation around them, the inhabitants of the ark are safe thanks to Noah and his consistent obedience.

After 40 straight days and nights, the pounding rain finally relents. Flood waters reach taller than the mountains. So deep is the flood that it takes 150 additional days for the water to subside. At this point the ark comes to rest on a mountain top. Soon the rest of the mountain tops become visible as the waters uncover the land below.

Noah sends a raven from the ark to see if the ground is dry enough to sustain life once again. The raven flies back and forth as there is still too much water for it to rest on dry ground. Later, a dove is sent out. It too can find no place to land so it returns to the ark. The following week, the dove is again sent and this time it returns with a freshly plucked olive leaf! Just like little tree buds are our first sign of new life each spring, this olive leaf is the first sign of life post-flood for Noah and his family.

Today, an olive branch is seen as a symbol of peace and reconciliation. To "hold out an olive branch" to someone is a metaphorical peace offering. Roots of this phrase can be traced back to Bible times when the dove brought Noah an olive leaf.

Now that the earth is dry, God invites Noah and his family and all the animals out of the ark and instructs them all to be fruitful and multiply on the earth. Noah builds an altar to the Lord to offer an animal sacrifice. God promises to never curse the ground again because of mankind—even though the intention of human hearts tend toward evil. God continues His promise offering consistent seed time and harvests—showing once more the importance God places on plants and trees.

God seals this promise with a sign: a rainbow. Each time there is a rainbow, God is remembering His promise to humans, and we humans have the opportunity to be grateful that God is being merciful in our lives today.

God in His infinite knowledge uses events like the flood to teach His people in multiple time periods. Noah and his family learn a lot about God during their lives. They see God is serious about requiring obedience. He is a master of what we call tough love. Noah learns that God rewards obedience. His life and the lives of his family members are spared due to his obedience to God. Noah also experiences the power of God's peace. While the outside world is in turmoil, Noah, his family, and the animals experience peace within the safety of the ark.

Today, we can also learn some important lessons about our God and the salvation He offers from the account of Noah and the flood. The idea of being brought safely through the water corresponds to the baptism we now receive to be saved through Christ (1 Peter 3:20-21). We will discuss this idea in more detail in future lessons.

We also see how hearts full of violence are detestable to God. If we are to be more like Noah and less like the people who are considered wicked, we need to have hearts at peace. But how do we do that? There are myriads of tips to achieve inner and outer peace, but what actually works? What creates lasting change and fosters the type of heart God desires from us?

In a ground-breaking book *The Anatomy of Peace*, the Arbinger Institute provides a framework for achieving peaceful hearts. The authors claim that humans like conflict and seek it. Most of you are probably shaking your heads at this absurd thought, because who in their right mind actually enjoys the brutality and the gut-wrenching pain of conflict?!?! However, this is the point the authors make: Most conflict is not caused by people in their right minds. Instead, they propose conflict comes when we betray ourselves and what we know is right. The uncomfortable feeling we get from self betrayal creates the need to justify our behavior. The authors provide helpful and effective advice to break the conflict cycle and live with a peaceful heart.[4] If you struggle with having a peaceful heart like those who were killed in the flood did, this book is worth a read!

The Bible is clear: If we want our intentions to be righteous in God's eyes as Noah's were, the olive branch of peace must be representative of our lives.

> *Whoever desires to love life*
> *and see good days,*
> *let him keep his tongue from evil*
> *and his lips from speaking deceit;*
> *Let him turn away from evil and do good;*
> *let him seek peace and pursue it.*
> *For the eyes of the Lord are on the righteous,*
> *and his ears are open to their prayer.*
> *But the face of the Lord is against those who do evil.*
> *– 1 Peter 3:10-12*

Prayer

Lord, at the sound of Your voice the world was made, and at Your command it was destroyed in a great flood. You are mighty and powerful but also full of mercy for those who love You and live according to Your will.

As we dive deep into the account of the flood, please grant us a firm understanding of Your will for us so that we have firm ground to stand on when the storms of life rise around us.

We are so grateful You keep Your promises, and we are reminded of them when we see rainbows in the sky. Thank You for Your peace and love.

In Jesus' mighty name,
Amen

1. Read Genesis 6–9. What do you find interesting or notable?

_____

_____

_____

_____

_____

2. How is mankind's relationship with God described in this account? (Genesis 6:5)

_____

_____

_____

3. How does God cleanse the world from the increasing corruption? (Genesis 6:17)

_____

_____

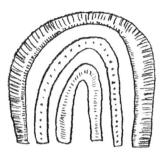

4. How does the idea of being buried in flood water relate to Jesus and our lives today? Read 1 Peter 3:20-21 for the answer.

_____

_____

_____

_____

5. What does God promise Noah? What's the symbol of the promise? (Genesis 9:8-15)

_____

_____

6. What can you do to have more peaceful intentions in your heart?

_____

_____

_____

_____

Under the Oak Grove

75 years old. The age for most of us when life is winding down. Careers have been had. Children raised. Friendships nurtured. Good in the world accomplished. However, for a man named Abraham, faith-filled adventures begin at age 75. God calls this man to leave the land he knew and the home he established to set off for an unknown place. What trust that must have required to trade stability for uncertainty. Abraham does not hesitate but sets off with his wife, his nephew, and all of their possessions.

When Abraham rests under the oak trees of Moreh, God once again chooses to meet man in the shade of the trees. The Lord appears to Abraham and promises the land he is living in will be given to his offspring.

While it would have been easy to doubt the feasibility of this promise, this 75-year-old man with no children instead chooses to worship and celebrate the promise from God. Thus begins the waiting game, a true test of patience.

Can Abraham patiently wait for God to fulfill His promises? If you read the entire account of Abraham, you will see that overall he trusts God. However, like any human, he has moments of weakness when his trust wavers and he tries to take matters into his own hands.

One of these moments of doubt led Sarah, who is still childless, to offer her Egyptian servant Hagar to her husband as a surrogate. Abraham consents to Sarah's request. Before long, Hagar is pregnant with Abraham's son. As expected, when humans try to take the place of God, a bigger mess is made. This pregnancy leads to bitterness between Sarah and her servant and later fosters bitterness between each of their sons. It can even be argued that the negative consequences of Sarah's grasp for control even extends to nations today.

Can you relate to the test of patience Abraham experienced? Life is full of waiting for both big and small things. We wait for doctors' appointments, for a potential job to call, for a soulmate, for children, for retirement, and we wait for the land of eternal rest that God has promised. Along the way, we need to exercise patience and different coping skills to restrain our immediate desires as we anticipate a bigger reward. Can we say no to tempting homemade pie in order to achieve a healthier weight? Can we pass up good "sales" at the store as we save for a house or a car? This ability is often referred to as delayed gratification and it is a practice that is essential to be successful in all areas of life.

In 1972, a famous study known as the Marshmallow Test was conducted at Stanford. A young child was offered a marshmallow by a researcher. The researcher told the child that they had to leave the room for a few minutes but would bring another marshmallow if the child waited to eat the first one. This study found that the longer the child was able to wait for the preferred reward (two marshmallows instead of one), the more likely this child would experience better life outcomes such as higher SAT scores, higher educational achievement, lower rates of obesity, and more. Similar experiments assured us that children are not doomed to an inferior life if they don't pass the so-called "Marshmallow Test." The ability to practice delayed gratification is now understood to be more of a muscle that can be strengthened rather than a trait you either have or don't.[5] That is good news for us, because faith in an eternal reward is the ultimate exercise in delayed gratification.

Abraham has plenty of opportunity to build his patience muscle and practice delayed gratification. He is around 75 years old when God first makes His promise to Abraham (Genesis 12). As each year goes by and his and his wife's bodies grow older, doubt threatens. They are past childbearing years, but God has promised a son. Will the promise this couple is clinging to be fulfilled?

Around 24 years after the original promise was made, once again God meets man in the shade of the trees. Under the oaks of Mamre, God renews a promise to a 99-year-old man named Abraham. He will have a son next year through whom future generations will be reconciled to God, first through the Jewish lineage, traditions, and law, and then ultimately through Jesus Christ.

If he had been a young man, this promise would have felt ripe with possibility. However, Abraham and his wife Sarah are old in age, well past childbearing years. So absurd is the thought of having a baby in her arms next year that Sarah laughs out loud when she hears the promise. Her laughter is met with reproach and a sobering question, "Is anything too hard for the Lord?" (Genesis 18:4). Indeed, nothing is too hard for God, as we see time and time again throughout the powerful accounts in God's holy Word.

As God promised, He visits Sarah (Genesis 21:1) and blesses her with a child. She conceives and becomes pregnant with a son. What an amazing image to picture the Lord Himself visiting a childless woman and granting her the ability to carry a precious soul in her once empty womb.

Sarah gives birth the following year to a son and names him Issac. Abraham is 100 years old when he is born. From this young boy, Abraham's family tree takes root. Its branches grow mightily over the years, and the lineage of Jesus' mother can be traced back to this young child of the promise.

Prayer

Our most faithful God, thank You for always keeping Your promises and giving us the most wonderful life to look forward to. Please strengthen us along our life's journey so we can say "no" to the things that will not help us accomplish our ultimate goal: to be reunited with You.

Remind us as we seek shelter under shady oaks in our own neighborhoods that the promise You made to Abraham long, long, ago still extends to us today.

Reassure us as we release our illusion of control that You already have everything worked out according to Your perfect and amazing plan.

In Jesus' faithful name,
Amen

1. Read Genesis 18:1-15 and Genesis 21. What do you find interesting or notable?

2. Read Genesis 13:14-18. This is God's covenant (or binding promise) to Abraham. Describe how the "seed" (or offspring) of Abraham will be blessed.

3. Read Galatians 3:29. Does Abraham's promise have anything to do with us today?

4. Abraham has two sons. Who is the son from the slave woman? (Genesis 21:9)

5. Why does Sarah want to drive out the son of the slave woman? (Genesis 21:10)

6. What can we learn about God from this account?

Caught in the Thicket

Have you ever been in a situation that seems impossibly hard? Thoughts twist and tangle into a mess and there is no clear way out. Fear and worry prick like thorns.

Abraham finds himself in one of these situations. In his old age, he and his wife Sarah are raising their dear son Issac, the child of God's promise. God calls Abraham to take his son (who is likely a young man) to a mountain to do the impossible: offer his only son as a sacrifice. This is simply a test of Abraham's faith, but Abraham does not know this is only a test. The weight of the request hangs heavy in his heart.

Can you imagine the confusion and fear that this request elicited? Abraham is old, his wife way past childbearing years, and now, the life of their only child is being called for. How can the promise of God be fulfilled if Isaac is dead? Can Abraham, who had waited what seemed like a lifetime for a son, give him up on an altar as God instructed?

The need for sacrifice is not a new concept to Abraham or Isaac. From the world's first sin back in the garden, innocent blood was shed as a consequence. The Old Law (which we read about soon) requires a sacrifice for sin, because "without the shedding of blood, there is no forgiveness" (Hebrews 9:21). But never before in the history of the world had God called for a human life to be sacrificed.

Imagine the dread that fills Abraham's heart as he and his son set out with everything they need. On the top of the mountain, Isaac finally notices something is missing: the lamb to be sacrificed. He asks his father where it is. The Bible doesn't tell us if Abraham's voice tearfully caught in his throat or if he answered with the peace only God can provide. Abraham's answer demonstrates so much faith when he replies simply to his son, "God will provide" (Genesis 22:8).

Abraham carefully prepares the altar. Sill, no lamb is in sight. He binds his son and puts him on the altar. By this point Isaac must realize what was going on. However, there appears to be no struggle. Both father and son are in full submission to God. Abraham, no doubt filled with both dread and faith, raises his knife to sacrifice his one and only son. An angel of the Lord immediately calls out and tells him to stop. As Abraham looks up, he sees a ram caught in the thicket. The boy and his father offer up this ram as a burnt offering to the Lord and God blesses Abraham again. What gratefulness must have filled Abraham's heart as he brings his only son home.

This account might raise the question: Is our God a God of human sacrifice? No. God over and over condemns nations for their practice of human sacrifice. The accounts in Deuteronomy 18:10, Deuteronomy 21:31, and Jeremiah 32:35 are a few examples. God, through the Law, forbids the Israelites from offering their children to a god that nations around them served (Leviticus 18:21). If God doesn't approve of child sacrifice, why put Abraham through this fearful situation? This account is shared to introduce a key aspect of our salvation: an only son willingly being offered up as a sacrifice for sin, once and for all. As we later see it is God—not man—who offers His only Son for our sin, once and for all.

Throughout his life and especially in this account, Abraham demonstrates an incredible amount of faith in God, and through that, freedom from the worry that so easily entangles human minds. Just like the thickets that trapped the ram, worry and anxiety create mental thickets that trap us from living the life God intends. Abraham bravely shows us the antidote to the plague of anxiety that has taken hold in the minds of both the young and the old. But before we dive into the antidote, we need to understand the scope of the problem.

In fear-inducing situations (such as the one Abraham and Isaac find themselves in), the human brain naturally goes into "fight or flight" mode. Rational, calm thoughts are switched off and the amygdala brain region (which responds emotionally, not rationally) takes over, hijacking the rest of the brain. This is why fears and anxiety feel so palatable, real, and completely rational when we are experiencing them. Then, as the situation deescalates, our calming bodies allows our brains to flip the switch back to a rational thought processes.[6]

If this is a natural process, what hope do we have to remain clear-minded when fear strikes like it undoubtedly did for Abraham? The trick to staying calm and in control in fearful situations lies in knowing how to "flip the switch" back to our rational brains quickly. Thankfully God has given us all we need to overcome fear and find peace in tense situations. Think of the amygadala as a smoke alarm. In a house, when the smoke alarm goes off, we check to see if there is a fire or if, perhaps, the steam from cooking or low batteries have simply triggered the alarm. If there is no actual fire, we turn the smoke alarm off. The same is true with our emotional "smoke alarm." We first survey the situation. Are we actually in danger or is worry or fear triggering our response? If we find no real and present danger, we need to turn the smoke alarm off. We do this by calming our bodies. Deep breathing allows our breath and heart rate to return to normal, thereby "flipping the switch" and allowing our rational brains to regain control.

Abraham, through calm, rational thinking, finds peace in a fearful situation by remembering that God faithfully keeps His promises. Abraham was promised a family line through Isaac, and so Abraham concludes that even if Isaac dies, God had the power to raise him up (see Hebrews 11:19). What amazing faith!

Just like Abraham is able to thoughtfully and rationally reason once he calmed down his "fight or flight" response, we too can calm our bodies to calm our minds in order to find the true peace that God so graciously provides.

Prayer

Oh God of peace and mercy, we are grateful for You. Just like the ram was stuck in a thicket, we ourselves get stuck in mental thickets. Our worried thoughts turn fearful and we lose sight of the truth that grounds us. Please help us control our thoughts and our bodies so we can be calm like Abraham was in stressful situations. We too want to stand firm and grounded in Your peace while troubles and hard times twist and tangle around us.

Thank You for being willing to sacrifice Your son, just as Abraham was willing to sacrifice his. We are forever grateful for Your love.

In Jesus' faithful name,
Amen

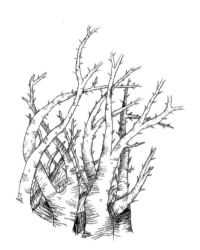

1. Read Genesis 22:1-19. What do you find interesting or notable?

2. How does God test Abraham? (Genesis 22:1-2)

3. Isaac asks his father where the lamb is. What is Abraham's response? (Genesis 22:7-8)

4. What does the angel say to Abraham when he went to sacrifice Isaac? (Genesis 22:12)

5. What does Abraham find caught in the thicket? (Genesis 22:13)

6. How does God put an end to blood sacrifices once and for all? (See Hebrews 10:12.)

7. What can we learn about God from this account?

When There Is No Harvest

We all have seasons in life that are filled to the brim with abundance and seasons where something or everything seems to have run dry. Maybe it's patience, maybe it's money, or maybe it's faith. Whatever it is that is lacking, seasons of famine range from challenging to downright devastating.

Joseph, Isaac's grandson, finds himself alternating back and forth between peaceful seasons of plenty and challenging seasons of famine during his life. His story begins with plenty. He is one of 12 brothers, and he is his father's favorite son. With this favorable position comes special treatment, gifts, and love, which creates extreme resentment and even hatred from the rest of his brothers.

Joseph's first low season comes directly after a wonderfully high one. His dad gifts Joseph a beautiful coat made with many colors. Back in that day, such a coat was indeed special as it took a lot of extra work to dye fabric and combine a variety of colors into a single garment. Joseph must have felt secure in his father's love each time he wrapped the coat around his young shoulders. Shortly after receiving this gift, Joseph is sent to check on his brothers who were tending sheep in the family's pasture. It's not challenging to imagine the disdain his brothers feel when they see their father's favorite arriving with yet another token of the love they so desperately yearn for.

So intense is their jealousy that they begin plotting how to get rid of this boy who is stealing too much of the limelight and love. They plot to kill Joseph and throw his body in a pit, but one of his brothers has mercy on the boy and suggests they not shed any blood but simply throw him into a pit. This brother intends to come back, rescue the boy, and return him to his father.

When Joseph arrives, his brothers maliciously rip off his special coat and throw him in a pit. With Joseph trapped in the pit, the other brothers sit down for lunch. As they are enjoying their food, a caravan of Ishmaelites (those descended from Abraham and his slave) approaches. The brothers decide killing Joseph would be of no benefit to them, so instead they sell him. The slave traders take Joseph with them and sell him to an Egyptian family. At the young age of 17, Joseph is cruelly ripped away from his family, his people, and the only life he ever knew. Worst of all, the pain and this terrible situation is brought about by his very own brothers.

Once in Egypt, through difficult hardships and God-given opportunities, Joseph rises to power. However, before the good times, Joseph finds himself at another absolute low. He is wrongly imprisoned for a crime he never committed and promptly forgotten about in a dark, dank prison. Instead of giving up, he holds fast to his faith and is rewarded with another season of plenty. He interprets Pharaoh's dream that foretold of seven years of bountiful harvest followed by seven years of severe famine. Joseph is promoted to second in command under Pharaoh himself. Under Joseph's leadership, Egypt is prepared for the famine. Neighboring countries are not.

When the famine becomes severe, Jacob hears there is grain in Egypt. He sends his sons to buy some. Joseph recognizes his brothers, but they do not recognize him.

After some intense drama and bargaining, Joseph reveals himself to his brothers and they are tearfully reunited and past wrongs are forgiven. A family is restored!

Joseph deeply desires to see his beloved father and makes arrangements as the famine worsens to bring his entire family to settle nearby. This is how the Israelites end up in the land of Egypt. Joseph's family thrives for many years with the approval and encouragement of the pharaoh under which Joseph served. Joseph's account, which began with familial betrayal, ends in forgiveness and reconciliation.

During Joseph's life, circumstances waver quickly between times of plenty and times of want, but we see Joseph hold fast to a mindset of abundance. What does that mean? There are two basic mindsets with which we can choose to approach life: a scarcity mindset or an abundance mindset.

A scarcity mindset is focused on the idea that there are not enough resources so it is necessary to hold on tight to what you have and seek to gain more for yourself.[7] This mindset causes one to see others as competition and causes one to operate out of fear. A scarcity mindset hijacks our thinking and prioritizes our unfulfilled needs. Joseph's brothers are a great example of a scarcity mindset. In their eyes, there is not enough of their father's love to go around so the biggest "threat" needs to be removed. The scarcity mindset impacts the thinking and decision making of these young men and leads them to do something awful—to sell their brother into slavery.

The opposite of a scarcity mindset is an abundance mindset, which is focused on the idea that there is plenty for all and there is no need to compete because of the abundance of resources. This mindset looks for the win-win opportunities and approaches life full of gratitude. An abundance mentality has been linked to better decision making, greater confidence in life, and more naturally embodies a growth mindset, which leads to increased success in all areas of life.[7]

Joseph's perspective is a good example of an abundance mindset. Despite the challenges he faces, he approaches new people and opportunities with confidence and hope instead of fear. Bad circumstances do not defeat him, and he shares abundance with an entire nation because of it.

Looking at the accounts we have studied so far, into which mindset would you place each of the characters? Why?

God greatly encourages us to choose the abundance mindset:

> *God is able to bless you abundantly, so that in all things at all times,*
> *having all that you need, you will abound in every good work.*
> –2 Corinthians 9:8

> *For God gave us a spirit not of fear but of power and love and self-control.*
> –2 Timothy 1:7

Prayer

Dear God who always provides, thank You for accounts like Joseph's who give us an example to follow as our lives reach thrilling highs and occasionally sink to heartbreaking lows.

Please help those who are currently suffering in a season where there is no "grain." Whether it be a lack of hope, or love, or resources, comfort those who are in need and remind them that You provide through all seasons of life.

As Joseph cultivated an attitude of plenty, please give us the strength and courage to do the same.

In Jesus' bountiful name,
Amen

1. Read Genesis 41-42. What do you find interesting or notable?

2. What does Pharaoh's dream mean? (Genesis 41:25-32)

3. What does Pharaoh believe sets Joseph apart from other men? (Genesis 41:37-39)

4. How and when does Joseph prepare for the famine? (Genesis 41:46-49)

_____

_____

_____

5. Read Genesis 45:4-6. How does Joseph explain that God used his brothers' bad intentions for ultimate good?

_____

_____

_____

6. What can we learn about surviving our own seasons of "famine" from this account?

_____

_____

_____

Hope from the Bulrushes

Mothers across cultures love to share their birth stories—the painful, joyous, intensely transformative event when new life bursts forth. That special moment when both a new baby and a new mother are born—facing the world that is to come. For most, these birth stories end in joy and celebration, but not for all. In fact, there was an entire generation of women in the Bible who lived through a time of devastating birth horrors.

A few generations after Joseph, there is a new pharaoh in Egypt that does not look favorably on Joseph's descendants. Pharaoh fears the Hebrews will become too powerful and rebel, fighting for their freedom. To combat this risk, Pharaoh boldly signs an edict ordering all Hebrew baby boys age two and under to be killed. It's hard to even imagine the fear, heartbreak, and unending grief these families faced.

Imagine the stifled sounds of secret labor, muffled cries from innocent babes, and the stolen moments when Hebrew families hold their precious boys before they are forcibly taken and killed.

Caught between a rock and a hard place, a young mother named Jochebed finds herself in a seemingly impossible situation. She secretly gives birth to a little baby boy and makes a risky yet brave decision that will change the outcome of an entire nation.

Jochebed values the life of her special child and keeps him hidden for three months. What faith and courage this must have taken as her family hid this baby, listening for signs of Egyptians around their house. During this time, exhausted and postpartum, Jochebed hatches a daring plan to save her son against all odds. She takes a papyrus basket (referred to as an "ark" in the original language) and carefully lines it with pitch to make it watertight. Placing her secret baby boy in it, she hides the basket among the bulrushes at the river's edge. Jochebed sends her older daughter Miriam to keep watch on the child. Imagine the prayers that are offered up that this child might be rescued from the river by a kind friend and not a deadly foe.

Pharaoh's daughter goes to the river to bathe and finds this child. She knows at once it is one of the babies destined for death under her father's harsh edict. However, in an act of great mercy, she pulls this child out of the water and decides that she will raise him as her own son. Then out steps Miriam, the child's older sister. She offers to find a woman to nurse the baby and when Pharaoh's daughter agrees, Miriam returns home with her precious brother in her arms. It's easy to imagine Jochebed's immense joy of not only knowing her son is spared but also having the unexpected honor of raising him until he is weaned (probably between 2-5 years old).

Psychology has shown the early years of a child set the tone for the rest of his or her life. Loving, secure attachment between a parent and child in the first two years predicts an adult's ability to cope with stress, develop empathy, social competence, self-esteem, emotional regulation, career success, leadership qualities, and more.[8] What a blessing it is for Jochebed to have these early years to lovingly shape the young man this child will grow up to become.

As heart-wrenching as it is to place her son in the arms of another woman, there is also a hope that other Hebrew mothers didn't have. Hope that her child will live. Hope that her child can now dream of a future. Hope that her child will carry the deep-seeded love of his family with him in his heart as he is raised and trained by their enemy, their oppressors.

The young child named Moses is granted the privileges of fine food, education, and the upbringing of royalty. Moses has the best the world had to offer, yet we see the Lord instilled a strong discerning spirit in this man. After serving Pharaoh for many years, Moses sees a Hebrew slave being mistreated. Instead of taking sanctuary into his adopted position of power and safety, he takes a huge risk and bravely protects the Hebrew. In his zeal, Moses kills the Egyptian who was mistreating the Hebrew slave. Once word gets out of this murder, Moses flees to land of Midian.

Moses once again acclimates to a new culture and a new people, making his home amongst the Midianites. He finds favor with a man named Reuel (also called Jethro) and marries one of his daughters. They are blessed with two sons.

Moses lives a quiet life with his family working as a herdsman. Imagine his surprise when one day, Moses hears a voice calling his name. As he looks for the source, Moses sees a bush that is consumed by fire, yet not burning up. He approaches this odd sight to get a closer look when a voice speaks from the bush telling him to take his sandals off because where he is standing is holy ground.

Moses has his first one-on-one conversation with our Almighty God that day. God informs Moses that he has been chosen to lead God's people (the Hebrews) out of Egyptian slavery and into the land God has promised. Moses is not interested in this position or proposition and comes up with excuse after excuse why God should choose someone else. However, God doesn't accept "no" for an answer. He created Moses, and despite Moses' fears, God knows his heart, his capabilities, and the impact Moses could have if he is willing to do what God is equipping him to do. Moses finally consents.

With his brother Aaron at his side, the powerful duo approaches Pharaoh and they demand freedom for God's people. (Note that up until now God's people were called Hebrews as Abraham was a Hebrew and God's people are descendants of the promise God made to Abraham. From here on out they are also referred to as the Israelites or the nation of Israel. Later, they are also called Jews or the Jewish people.)

Freedom is hardly granted without struggle, and this instance is no different. Pharaoh refuses to let the Israelites go, and God counters with terrible plagues. Each plague is removed when Pharaoh promises freedom, but when Pharaoh changes his mind, a new plague descends on the people. This back and forth culminates in the 10th plague: death of the firstborn son of each family. The Hebrews who sacrifice a lamb without blemish and smear the blood on their door are spared this terrible fate. (Again, note the important theme of blood, sacrifice, and a lamb without blemish!)

At midnight, cries of distress ring out from the Egyptian houses as each one discovers their firstborn had died. Pharaoh summons Moses and Aaron in the night and commands all the Israelites leave immediately. About 600,000 men plus women, children, flocks and herds leave Egypt that night. The Lord leads them with a pillar of fire to provide light during the night and a pillar of cloud during the day. Can you imagine what a sight that must have been?

Meanwhile, after the initial shock and grief, Pharaoh again has a change of heart as he realizes he let his forced labors walk away. He pursues the Israelite people with chariots, horses, and his imposing army. The Israelites see their former oppressors coming in full force from behind. In front of them stands an impassable body of water known as the Red Sea. God's people, forgetting who it is that fights for them, begin to panic.

Right then and there, God again shows His mighty power. He parts the waters of the Red Sea and His people walk through the sea on dry ground with a wall of water on each side! (Note the theme of passing through water to be saved!) When the Egyptians charge in pursuit, the water falls and engulfs them, leaving the Israelites free once again.

The thrill of victory soon subsides as the people wander in the wilderness without sources of water or food. They grumble against Moses. However, despite their lack of faith, God continues to provide for His people. He brings forth water from a rock and sends "bread from heaven" to feed the hungry people.

After about three months of wilderness wandering, the Israelites come to a mountain known as Mount Sinai. With great thunder and lighting, God powerfully descends on the mountain in blazing fire. Imagine seeing smoke all around, feeling the earth shake beneath your feet, and hearing the sound of trumpets filling the air. It must have been a terrifying site for those who were at the foot of that mountain. The people are rightfully in awe and intimidated of the power of their mighty God.

God calls Moses to the top of the mountain for another one-on-one encounter. During this time, God gives Moses the Law, the set of rules and commandments that His people will live by.

The Law is the basis of the Jewish religion. It outlines what sin is and the on-going, yearly sacrifices required to make amends for sin. It helps set the stage for God's people to understand their need for a sacrifice. "Without the shedding of blood, there is no forgiveness" (Hebrews 9:21).

Prayer

Lord, just as the young baby was drawn out of the water and given life, we pray that the true meaning of Your words are drawn out of the pages of Your holy Word as we study this powerful account of a woman with courageous love and a son who refused to forsake his true family.

Lord, as we examine our own hearts, grant us clear sight through the "bulrushes" in our lives and remove the things that obscure our view of Your love and grace.

Help us to understand the things that oppress and challenge us won't last forever, and You are a God of freedom. Lead us to the Promised Land.

In Jesus' saving name,
Amen

1. Read Exodus chapters 2 and 3. What do you find interesting or notable?

_____

_____

_____

_____

_____

2. Does anyone hear the Israelites cry for help? (Exodus 2:23-25)

_____

_____

3. Who does God say He is? (Exodus 3:13-15). What does that mean to you?

_____

_____

_____

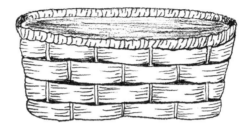

4. What do God's people put on their doors to be spared death? (Exodus 12:13-14)

5. How do the Israelites get across the Red Sea? What can we learn from this account? (Exodus 14:13-22)

6. Where does God give Moses what becomes known as the Law? (Exodus 19:16-20)

7. The Israelites alternate between faith and doubt in God. Can you relate?

Orchards You Didn't Plant

When we work hard and earn something, we often feel the sense of pride and accomplishment that comes along with achievement. However, it's difficult to describe the immense gratitude and the humbling feeling of awe when we are handed an absolutely breathtaking gift that we don't deserve but are being given anyway. Such is the blessing the Israelites received when God promises them a bountiful land cultivated by others.

Armed with the Law and guided by God Himself, Moses and the Israelites continue their long, winding journey through the desert. In the dry, arid space far away from distractions, God slowly reminds His people who He is and lets them get re-acquainted with His expectations as well as His mercy. When they are hungry and thirsty, God hears their groaning and provides. When the Israelites grow arrogant and disobedient, God offers discipline and redirection. When the Israelites are scared, God sees their fear and fills them with hope and courage. Day in and day out, God is there in both big and small ways, leading His people faithfully to the Promised Land.

What should have been a short journey turns into an extraordinary one. When the Israelites are on the brink of reaching the Promised Land, Moses sends 12 spies out to gather information about the people whom they will need to conquer in order to take possession of the Promised Land. These 12 spies have witnessed the 10 plagues, crossed the Red Sea on dry ground, eaten bread from heaven, drank water from a rock, and watched God grant victory after victory. These spies see the richness of the land that lay before them. It is everything they imagined and more — abundant crops, oversized fruits, milk, and honey. But one thing stands in their way — fear. The people of the land intimidate the Israelites. Instead of considering God's mighty hand, they shy away from the opportunity of a lifetime. After spying on the inhabitants of the Promised Land, 10 of the 12 spies report that it will be better to stay in the desert instead of taking possession of the land. Sometimes we find it easier to doubt our own abilities rather than trust God and taste His sweet and promised victory. Our hope is hindered by our fear.

Imagine the frustration and anger that burned in God—to have offered such a breath-taking gift, only to have it flatly refused by an ungrateful nation. Such a disregard for God does not come without consequence. Not one man over the age of 20 will be allowed to enter the Promised Land except the two spies, Joshua and Caleb, who fully trust in God.

Thus begins the Israelites' desert wandering. For 40 years they wander, waiting out the consequence of their doubt. Their journey could have been made in about two weeks, but instead, God leads them in a long, meandering route so they have plenty of time to consider what choice they will make the next time God presents them with an opportunity.

The faithful young spy Joshua becomes Moses' assistant and is later appointed by God to be his successor to lead the Israelites into the Promised Land. Joshua, with the power of God, proves to be a military leader to contend with. Enemies fall before him as Israel advances on the Promised Land. With victory in sight, Joshua gives a powerful speech to the people in which he demands they make a choice whom they are going to serve. Joshua boldly declares that he and his house will serve the Lord.

Joshua had witnessed firsthand how easily the people were swayed, and unfortunately, research shows that we are no smarter in our decision-making today than the Israelites were back then. A study was conducted with 50 U.S. college students who volunteered to participate in a "vision" test. Each participant was placed in a room with seven other individuals who appeared to be volunteers. However, these seven individuals were part of the study and had instructions to unanimously give the wrong answer to an obvious question so psychologists could study the impact of social pressure on choices. The experiment showed a target line and asked participants to select which line (A, B, or C) was identical to the target.

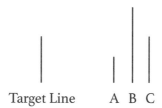

Target Line   A B C

Over the span of 12 clinical trials, 75% of participants conformed to the obviously wrong answer at least once. When these participants were interviewed, psychologists questioned what led them to choose the wrong answer. They found there were two main reasons: participants wanted to fit in, or they felt the group was better informed than they were.[9]

As the Israelites enter the Promised Land, it is full of wonderful blessings, but it is also bursting with different ideology, gods, and a conflicting way of life. God knows the Israelites will be tempted by the same two social pressures we still feel today: to fit in to what seems normal and to hold the knowledge of others in higher regard than what we know ourselves to be true. Joshua stands before the people and presents them with a choice — the same choice we are given today:

> ...*Choose this day whom you will serve, whether the gods your fathers served in the region beyond the River, or the gods of the Amorites in whose land you dwell. But as for me and my house, we will serve the Lord.*
> –Joshua 24:15

Will we conform to the beliefs of our families or our cultures or choose God? May we be as bold as Joshua and declare that we and our houses will serve the Lord!

Consider the impact of choosing the Lord. A people who were brutally oppressed in slavery are now free. A people with no place to call their own now have land. A people who had spent 40 years in a dry, desolate place now have a prosperous inheritance. A people who labored in vain for another nation receive the bounty of someone else's labor. There is much we can learn from the Israelites and their journey to the Promised Land, but perhaps, one of the most important lessons is how it applies to us today. Just as God made a promise to Abraham to give his offspring an inheritance (Genesis 12), God has made us a new promise through His son Jesus Christ to prepare a place for us once we have journeyed through the wilderness of this life. With faith and obedience, we too can enter the ultimate rest that God promises His people (Hebrews 4:1-11).

Prayer

Lord, thank You for the account of the Israelites. From their triumphs and tragedies, we can learn how to successfully navigate the wilderness in our own lives. As You have set us free from slavery to sin and death, we look forward to entering Heaven — the Promised Land You have prepared for us.

Just like the Israelites, we too stand at a crossroads where a choice is required. Give us the strength to withstand the masses in the land where we are living and refuse to follow their "gods." Don't allow us be mastered by fear. Help us courageously step out and be different. We might get ridiculed. We might be treated differently, but You, God, are worth it.

In Jesus' mighty name,
Amen

1. Read Joshua 24. What do you find interesting or notable in this chapter?

2. Why do you think God reminds His people of all He has done so far?

3. When does Joshua ask the people to choose whom they will serve? (Joshua 24:15)

4. What reasons do the Israelites give for choosing to serve God? (Joshua 24:16-18)

5. Joshua warns the people not to make this promise lightly because of the nature of God. How does Joshua describe God? (Joshua 24:19-20)

6. What does Joshua place as a witness to their promise? (Joshua 24:25-27)

7. What pressures do you feel to conform to the world and the people around you?

Trees Planted by Streams of Water

Unfortunately, the Israelites are not deeply rooted in their convictions and continue to have a hot and cold relationship with God. They are easily swayed by the nations around them as Joshua feared they would be. God appoints judges to lead the people and these men and women are charged with the seemingly impossible task of drawing people back to God. During this time, much like today, truth and morals appear completely subjective — everyone does what is right in their own eyes (Judges 21:25).

God's people fail to honor God as the King and beg for an earthly king like the neighboring nations. They do not want to be led by judges. With a stern warning (I Samuel 8:9), God grants their request and appoints Saul as king. When King Saul ignores God's rules, God hands the kingdom to a young man named David. David's accounts are full of amazing feats and heartbreaking betrayals. Yet, his desire to serve God despite his shortcomings lead David to be known as a "man after God's own heart" (I Samuel 13:14). David's devotion is rewarded as God renews His vow with David, promising David will never fail to have a descendant sit on the throne.

I have made a covenant with my chosen;

I have sworn to David my servant,

"I will establish your seed forever,

and build up your throne

to all generations."

–Psalms 132:11

This promise that David's "seed" will be established forever is a renewal of the promise God made to Abraham as David descended from Abraham.

...And through your seed all nations on earth will be blessed,

because you have obeyed Me.

–Genesis 22:18

David is also known for writing many of the songs and poems recorded in the book of Psalms. David called out to God in his anguish and praised God during good times. Psalms is part of the Bible that is considered "wisdom literature," which means it contains wise sayings and advice that can be used to live according to God's will.

Psalm 1, which was written anonymously, uses plants and trees to proclaim the benefit of being in unity with God. It tells us that those who meditate on God's words are like "trees planted by streams of water" (Psalm 1:2-3). What a beautiful image that is. Trees planted by a stable water source are able to be fed constantly, allowing them to grow tall and bear good fruit. The moist ground allows for deep sturdy roots that keep the tree strong and grounded when storms or winds threaten. On the other hand, those who aren't united with God are called "wicked" and are described like chaff that the wind drives away. Chaff refers to the loose, outer covering of grain that is either blown away by the wind or removed during harvest. It is the discarded part of the plant.

This vivid illustration presents each of us with a choice of what we are to become: a deeply rooted, fruit-bearing tree or invaluable chaff, blown away by the wind. What are you currently? What do you desire to be?

The idea of being deeply rooted often refers to how solid and steady a person is and his or her ability to withstand difficult times and bounce back from setbacks or even trauma. This powerful ability that Psalm 1 describes is known as resiliency. Resiliency plays a huge role in how successful we are, how happy we are, and how we handle life's inevitable setbacks.

Researchers around the world have been studying what determines an individual's level of resiliency and how to build resiliency. Here are some interesting facts:

- People who faced the greatest challenges showed the highest levels of resiliency. Overcoming challenges helps us grow![10]
- Resilience helps shield us from depression and anxiety.[10]
- Knowing one's family story and history is a strong predictor of resilience.[11] No wonder God wanted His children reminded of who they were and what they had already overcome!

While science and psychology can teach us a lot about being resilient, God in His infinite wisdom, gives us many examples in nature of what resiliency looks like.

In 2017 a deadly Category 5 storm ripped through Puerto Rico. It was the worst natural disaster recorded and the aftermath was widespread devastation. Experts from various fields were interviewed as the island and the world pondered how Puerto Rico would recover. The director of forestry Dr. Ariel Lugo was optimistic as he referenced the trees. Even though the powerful winds had ripped the leaves off all the trees, the Ceiba trees had already grown leaves back in just nine days.[12] To go from being completely stripped bare, branches broken and beat up by pounding rain, to new growth in a matter of just a few days is such a powerful example of resilience.

This is the life God desires for us. He knows there will be storms, sometimes devastating ones. We will face challenging hardships, heart-wrenching loss, broken relationships, financial stress or even ruin. There will be times we feel stripped bare and completely broken. But that is when strong roots make the difference between success and failure. If we are deeply rooted, we can bounce back. It might not be as fast as the Ceiba trees, but that's ok. Resiliency isn't a race but the ability to not stay stuck in a down-and-out position.

God grants us this beautiful gift of deep roots planted near a life-giving water source. We just have to choose it. As you read Psalm 1, picture yourself as that tree. What changes in your life need to be made in order to access this gift God is offering?

Prayer

Dear God, You are the giver of all life. With You, we can have life to the fullest. Thank You for making it so simple for us to access Your life-saving grace.

Please help us desire Your Word like trees desire fresh water. Allow Your Word to nourish us from our deep roots to the tips of our branches and firmly ground us in Your amazing truth.

As we meditate on Your Word, Lord, give us the strength and the resilience to withstand the many challenges that life inevitably brings.

In Jesus' name,
Amen

1. Read Psalm 1. What do you find interesting or notable in this Psalm?

2. What are the characteristics of a person who is blessed? (Psalm 1:1-3)

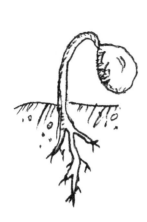 

3. What are the characteristics of a person that is called wicked? (Psalm 1:4-6)

_____

_____

_____

_____

4. What will happen to those who are considered wicked? (Psalm 1:5-6)

_____

_____

_____

5. What changes do you need to make in order to be more like a tree planted by streams of water?

_____

_____

_____

_____

Wisdom from the Trees

Nature is a powerful teacher. Ants teach us what hard work looks like. We see the power of consistency as a gentle stream of water slowly wears through a hard, unmovable boulder. The transformation of a caterpillar into a beautiful butterfly reminds us that we too have the ability to make something beautiful with our lives. We can learn so much from the trees with their deep roots, strong trunks, and flexible, fruit-filled branches.

In the world's first garden, we learned about the Tree of Life, a tree with life-giving fruit. The actual Tree of Life was blocked from mankind after sin in the garden to prevent mankind from living eternally with sin, but we see references to figural trees of life here in the book of Proverbs. The Tree of Life is mentioned again at the end of the Bible when we learn about how amazing, healing, and soul-sustaining Heaven will be.

Proverbs like Psalms is wisdom literature. It was written through God's divine inspiration by Solomon, King David's son. When David grows old, he passes his throne down to his son. Like any loving parent who sees his child on the brink of a task that will challenge him emotionally, physically, and spiritually, David shares advice to uplift and ground his son.

> *And you, Solomon my son, know the God of your father and serve Him with a whole heart and with a willing mind, for the Lord searches all hearts and understands every plan and thought. If you seek Him, He will be found by you, but if you forsake Him, He will cast you off forever. Be careful now, for the Lord has chosen you to build a house for the sanctuary; be strong and do it.*
> 1 Chronicles 28:9-10

What a charge to be given as a young leader! Yet David, through God's wisdom, knows the power of setting the bar high. Research has shown time and time again that when a teacher or parent expects enhanced performance from a child, that child will indeed rise to the occasion and deliver an enhanced performance.[13] Human behavior, perhaps more than we like to admit, is heavily influenced by what others believe we can or cannot do. It is so crucial that parents, educators, and leaders of any sort take note of David's powerful example and expect good things from those around us.

Solomon is handed the throne under the blessing and high expectations of his father and the approval of God Himself. All of Israel and David's warriors (known as David's mighty men) pledge their allegiance to Solomon, ensuring a peaceful transition of power. In addition, God blesses Solomon with earthly wealth and riches. Having the favor of God and all the people is a great way for a young king to step into power to begin his reign.

After his father's death, Solomon and all the people go to a high place to worship God. This is the first recorded act of Solomon's reign and shows Solomon is following in his father's footsteps by putting God first. That night, God appears to Solomon and says, "Ask what I shall give you." God, whose voice commanded the entire world into existence, is offering this young man anything he asks. Can you imagine the things that must have run through Solomon's mind? He could have riches, honor, power, never-ending military success, long life, or whatever else tickled his mind in the quiet moments.

What does he choose? Wisdom. The word *Chokmah* from the original Hebrew language means both knowledge and the ability to apply it. And what a powerful choice wisdom is for this young king! He asks God to give him wisdom to lead the nation of Israel that is under his charge. God is so pleased with this selfless decision He also grants Solomon more riches, possessions, and honor than any king had ever had or ever would have in the future.

Solomon successfully accomplishes the greatest task of his entire reign: building a house for the Lord. This place of worship was meticulously designed by God Himself; the plans given to David, who passed them down to Solomon. Yet Solomon wisely acknowledges that no human structure can house our mighty and all-powerful God. Instead, this temple was to be a place where God's eyes and ears are attentive to the requests His people (2 Chronicles 7:15).

With this monumental task behind him, Solomon turns his mind to other pursuits. He states in Ecclesiastes (another book he authored through God's inspiration) that he explored all the world had to offer: wisdom, folly, self-indulgence, projects, power, riches, sex, entertainment, and more. He boldly states that "all was vanity and a striving after wind, and there was nothing to be gained under the sun" (Ecclesiastes 2:11). In the end, the conclusion Solomon reaches is this: "Fear God and keep His commandments, for this is the whole duty of man" (Ecclesiastes 12:13). Isn't that amazing? The wisest man in the world, after experiencing all the world has to offer, comes back to the very same requirement that God charged Adam and Eve with beneath the trees in the world's first garden.

From this perspective, Solomon writes Proverbs, a collection of carefully chosen wise sayings intended to provide firm guidance in God's truth. The first nine chapters are written from a father to a son. Just like his father David set firm expectations, Solomon presents wisdom to his sons as highly desirable—something to be sought after and treasured. On the other hand, folly is described as something to avoid at all costs. Even though these proverbs are not written to us directly, the principles of these wise sayings can benefit us all!

As the author points us to wisdom (knowledge and the ability to use it effectively), notice how wisdom is often portrayed as a tree of life. If we act with God's wisdom, our lives will be a source of life to those around us. This takes us right back to where it all began in the world's first garden and points to an unknown time in the future where it will end when humans are reunited with their Maker and once again have access to the Tree of Life.

Prayer

Dear loving Father, just as David set high expectations for his son, You too set high expectations for us. Expectations to love one another, to follow You, and to seek and apply wisdom in all we do. Please aid us on our journey to accomplish the tasks You have laid before us in our lives. Help us to approach all that we do with strength of character and steadfast hope in You.

We see through these proverbs how powerful wisdom is and we too want to have more wisdom from You. Not so we can take pride in what we know, but so we can share Your truth with others. Please grant us increased wisdom and shield us from the temptations of folly.

In Jesus' saving name,
Amen

1. Why was Proverbs written? (See Proverbs 1:1-4)

_____

_____

_____

_____

_____

2. What are the benefits of wisdom? (See Proverbs 3:13-27)

_____

_____

_____

_____

_____

_____

3. What traits or actions are considered to be a "tree of life"?

Proverbs 3:17-18

Proverbs 11:30

Proverbs 13:12

Proverbs 15:4

4. What does it mean that the above traits or actions are a "tree of life"?

5. What benefits of wisdom listed in Proverbs 3 are most desirable to you? Why?

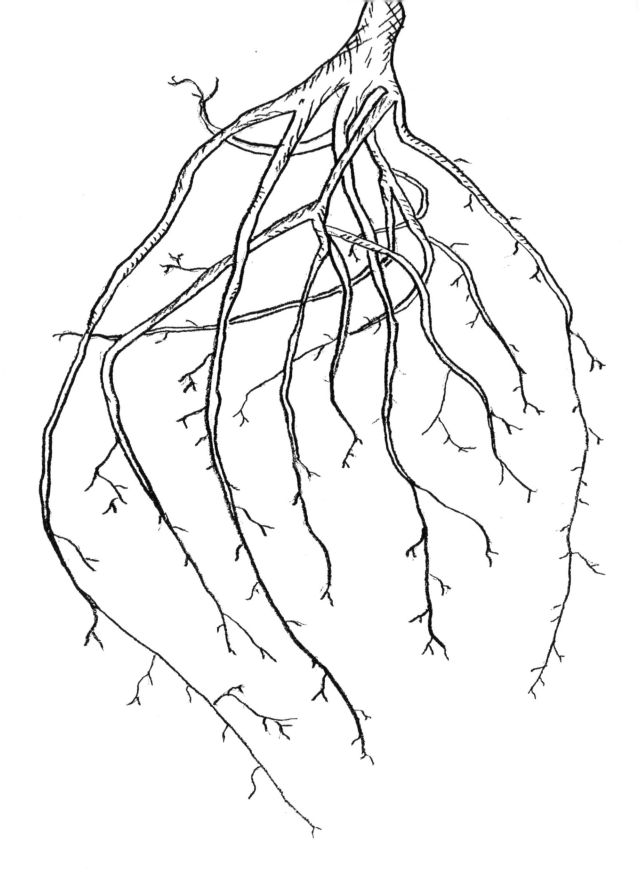

A Root out of Dry Ground

New growth bursts forth each spring as fertile ground, wet with fresh snow melt, supplies all seeds need to sprout green growth. In climates with adequate rainfall, these sprouts will grow into healthy, thriving plants and trees. But what about the arid regions? The same seeds with the same potential do not have the same success in all ecosystems.

Unfortunately, this same principle applies to humans. Children who are lucky enough to be born into families and communities blessed with abundant resources are more likely to reach higher potentials than their peers with access to less resources. Studies have found that children who live in poverty are less likely to graduate, attend schools with less academic opportunities, are more likely to be poor as adults, and suffer poorer health.[14] Money is not the only important resource. Studies also show children whose parents are less involved in their lives reach lower levels of success than their peers who have higher parental involvement.[15] Roots out of dry ground don't thrive like those springing forth from rich, fertile soil.

Is this a hard and fast rule of life? Thankfully no! There are amazing stories about men, women, young and old overcoming seemingly insurmountable barriers and succeeding against all odds. Perhaps the greatest success story of someone defying all odds can be found in the birth and life of our Savior.

Even more amazing is that Jesus' birth was predicted centuries before in great detail by multiple men known as prophets who spoke on behalf of God. Scholars have gone through the Bible and looked for all the prophecies (predictions) about Jesus Christ and checked carefully to see if they actually happened. There are over 300 prophecies made long before Jesus was born that He fulfilled while on earth. In the book *Science Speaks*, the authors show the likelihood of one man fulfilling only eight of the prophecies is 1 in 10^{17} power.[16] It is virtually impossible for 300 prophecies to be fulfilled by chance. This is further evidence of God's mighty hand working to save His people!

Recall the promise God first makes to Abraham then renews through David when He promises King David in 2 Samuel 7:16:

> *And your house and your kingdom shall be made sure forever before me.*
> *Your throne shall be established forever.*

If God was talking about an earthly kingdom, this prophecy would be a failed one. The family of Abraham and David is not ruling today on earth in Judah or anywhere else. Thankfully, God's promise is bigger than this life. This is confirmed years after Jesus Christ by one of the New Testament writers who speaks through the Holy Spirit in Galatians 3:16:

Now the promises were spoken to Abraham and to his seed. He does not say, "And to seeds," as referring to many, but rather to one, "And to your seed," that is, Christ.

Let's also consider a couple more prophecies that were made 600-700 years before Jesus was born. Below is a prophecy from Isaiah 53:2:

For He grew up before Him like a young plant,
and like a root out of dry ground;
He had no form or majesty that we should look at Him,
and no beauty that we should desire Him.

Nothing about the outward appearance of Jesus points to success. He comes from a family line that had just about fallen apart due to disobedience. His mother becomes pregnant as an unmarried teen. He is raised in a city not known for prophets or anything even good (John 1:46; John 7:52). He is not noticeably handsome. He doesn't have a distinguished career or family. The fact that Jesus becomes a prominent figure in history and the key figure in Christianity certainly defies all odds.

David's father Jesse is referred to as the stump of the family tree. David's grandsons and great grandsons ruled foolishly and David's kingdom was left in shambles when Isaiah makes the following prophesy in Isaiah 11:1:

A shoot will come up from the stump of Jesse;
from his roots a Branch will bear fruit.

Note the vivid tree imagery in these prophecies! Abraham's seed. A root out of dry ground. A stump that appears to hold little life will have a shoot that grows strong enough that its branch will bear fruit!

How do we know these prophecies are referring to Jesus? One way is through the books of the Bible that were written after Jesus' time on earth. In Romans 15:1-13 Paul, through divine inspiration, reveals "Christ confirmed the promises" God made to the patriarchs (the line of men from Abraham through which God established the nation of Israel) and quotes this prophecy from Isaiah.

The prophet Jeremiah, who was born around 100 years after Isaiah, foretold Jesus in a very similar manner in Jeremiah 23:5:

> *"Behold, the days are coming," declares the Lord,*
> *"When I will raise up for David a righteous Branch;*
> *And He will reign as king and act wisely*
> *And do justice and righteousness in the land."*

Again, God uses a tree as the way to describe His only Son, our wise King who rules eternally. Next time you are outside, look at the trees and remember how God's promise started with a small seed, grew into a tender shoot from an old trunk, and bears everlasting fruit!

Prayer

To our God, the great promise keeper, thank You for being 100% consistent with keeping Your Word. It allows us to feel secure in the promises You make to us.

We are also incredibly grateful that You are the God that swings impossible odds into our favor. You have helped countless "underdogs" do amazing things in Your name, and You help each of us overcome seemingly insurmountable challenges in our own lives.

Thank You for the trees. They remind us big things start with little seeds and tender shoots can grow into strong, fruit-bearing branches. Help us to be fruit-bearing in our lives.

In Jesus' name,
Amen

1. Read Isaiah 53. What do you find interesting or notable?

2. What are some ways Jesus is described in Isaiah 53?

3. How are we counted righteous through Jesus? (Isaiah 53:4-5 and 11-12)

4. Read Deuteronomy 18:18-22. Where do the words of a prophet come from?

_____

_____

_____

5. How can we know a prophet's words are from God? (Deuteronomy 18:18-22)

_____

_____

_____

6. Do you think using seeds, plants, and trees was a fitting way to announce the coming of the Messiah, Jesus Christ? Why or why not?

_____

_____

_____

_____

A Gnarled Family Tree

Do you have roots in England, Asia, India, or Africa? Can you trace your ancestors back hundreds of years? Do you pride yourself in coming from a long line of nobles, or do you find yourself cringing when you look at the sordid past of your bloodline? Our desire to know our roots can be shown in the number of people who use sites designed to trace ancestry. God understands our desire to link our present lives to the past and those who came before us. It's grounding to know whose shoulders we are standing on.

Perhaps that is why the good news of Jesus Christ's birth begins with His family tree in Matthew 1. One might expect the Savior of the world would have a royal, impeccable bloodline, but the exact opposite is true. Jesus' bloodline, which can be traced back to Adam and Eve in the world's first garden, includes liars, prostitutes, a murderer, foreigners, an adulteress, an evil king, and more. The fact that God can use imperfect people for His perfect plan should give us all hope! Even more incredible is the fact that we are all invited to be grafted into Jesus Christ's life-giving family tree!

Jesus' earthly life begins in the womb of an unsuspecting teen named Mary. The young virgin is engaged, but not married yet. Imagine her shock when an angel visits her and tells her she is carrying God's holy Son. An angel also visits her soon-to-be husband to quell his fears that his fiancé had been unfaithful to him.

The two marry. Near the time of Mary's due date, the couple travels to Bethlehem (Joseph's hometown) for a census. It was customary in first-century Palestine for relatives to house each other in a spare room, often translated as an "inn."[17] This spare room was typically an upper room on the second floor. The main floor contained the family's living quarters as well as an area where their animals could be brought in each night. In this space, there were hollows in the ground filled with hay to feed the animals.[18] So many family members are in town for the census that there is no room for Mary and Joseph in the spare room or "inn," so they stay in the area where animals are housed at night. Without fancy accommodations, the Son of God is born humbly, changing lives forever.

The Bible doesn't provide much information about the early life of Jesus. However, we can learn a lot from what Jesus does publicly right before He begins His ministry to share the good news of salvation. Jesus is baptized. In the original language this literally means being immersed or dunked in water. The Law of Moses had some instructions for ritual cleansing with water (Exodus 30:17-21), but the idea of full body immersion is introduced right before Jesus' ministry began by a man who became known as John the Baptist.

The same prophets who announced the Savior would be born also foretold the life and purpose of John the Baptist (Isaiah 43). John the Baptist is born about six months before Jesus was and he is sent to prepare the way for Jesus. John preaches baptism for the sake of repentance (turning away from sin). In Matthew 3:11 he said,

I baptize you with water for repentance, but He who is coming after me is mightier than I, whose sandals I am not worthy to carry. He will baptize you with the Holy Spirit and fire.

Jesus does not need to be saved from sin as He is perfect (1 John 3:5). In baptism, Jesus models a crucial step in reuniting with God. God Himself speaks from Heaven immediately after Jesus' baptism, saying He is pleased with His Son. As further confirmation of Jesus' divine calling, God sends His Holy Spirit upon Jesus. When we are baptized into Christ, God sends His Holy Spirit to us as the confirmation of our belonging and future inheritance (Acts 2:38; Ephesians 1:13-14).

After Jesus' baptism, the Spirit leads Jesus to the wilderness where He spends 40 days fasting. During this time the devil tempts Him and angels attend to Him. When the 40 days are over, Jesus returns to Galilee proclaiming the Gospel (the good news) and calling for repentance. Along the way, Jesus heals many and calls men to follow Him as disciples (learners). Some of these men are given special power from God to help confirm Jesus' message. Matthew, Mark, Luke, and John, guided by the Holy Spirit, record Jesus' life, ministry, death, and resurrection. Their books are often called the Gospels. These eyewitness accounts overlap greatly as they are all sharing similar accounts from slightly different perspectives.

Matthew is a tax collector. His Gospel focuses on how Jesus fulfills the Old Law given by Moses. Mark is a member of the early church and is instrumental in spreading the Gospel through missionary trips. He records events thematically. Luke is a doctor. In his meticulously organized account, there is an emphasis placed on Jesus' power to heal. John was a fisherman before Jesus calls him. John spends significant time with Jesus and is very specific about his goal when sharing the Gospel:

> *Now Jesus did many other signs in the presence of the disciples, which are*
> *not written in this book; but these are written so that you may believe that*
> *Jesus is the Christ, the Son of God, and that by believing you may have*
> *life in His name.*
> -John 20:30-31

Each of these men were inspired by God to write these accounts, which is why there are no errors or discrepancies. Humans tend to be unreliable as eyewitnesses as memory is malleable and inconsistent. A group called The Innocence Project found that over 70% of convicted criminals in 130 cases they overturned were wrongfully convicted due to faulty eyewitness accounts.[19] Age, vision, stress, skin color, and leading questions are contributing factors that can lead to eyewitness accounts being unreliable.

From a human standpoint, men who come from different backgrounds, are subjected to different stressors, and have different goals would be expected to be unreliable in their reporting of Jesus' life. But this is not the case! The reliability of their accounts speaks to divine inspiration as the Bible itself claims (2 Timothy 3:16-17).

Prayer

Heavenly Father, thank You for demonstrating time and time again that You can bring beauty from our ashes. It is a comfort to know that You saw fit to bring salvation into this world through Your perfect Son, born from a bloodline of imperfect people. As we look at our own families, the triumphs and failures, help us to see Your grace and mercy through it all.

We are so grateful for the Gospel, the good news of the salvation You offer to each of us. The eyewitness accounts of Matthew, Mark, Luke, and John provide such hope and encouragement as we navigate difficult situations and try to live more like Jesus commands.

In Jesus' saving name,
Amen

1. Read Mark 1. What do you find interesting or notable?

2. What message does John the Baptist preach? (Mark 1:4-8)

3. What happens when Jesus is baptized? (Mark 1:9-11)

4. How can we receive the gift of the Holy Spirit? (Acts 2:38)

5. What are some of the roles of the Holy Spirit?

John 14:26

Romans 8:26

John 16:13

John 14:16

Romans 8:14

Titus 3:5-6

6. Who tempts Jesus? (Mark 1:12-13)   Why is Jesus tempted? (Hebrews 2:18)

Fruit of Repentance

Life comes in seasons. There are seasons of new growth and seasons of renewal. Seasons where everything appears quiet and dormant and seasons where new opportunities burst forth like flowers after a quenching spring rain. It can be hard to watch others whose lives appear in full bloom at a time when your own life feels dead and dormant. But take heart! Just like each fruit has its own season, we too have unique seasons in which we will bear fruit.

Consider the papaya tree. It is one of the fastest growing trees. In six short months, it goes from a tiny seed in the dirt to a strong fruit-bearing tree![20] While it is growing, changes can be seen almost daily. On the far opposite is the mangosteen. This slow growing tree takes 15+ years to bear fruit.[21] Decades go by with little evidence of the fruit that is to come. Fruit from different trees also varies widely. Blueberries are tiny, each weighing only half a gram. Jackfruit, the largest fruit, can weigh 100 lbs.[22] Durian, known as the king of fruit, has unmistakable odor.[23] Various trees come to produce delicious fruit, but the taste, timing, and the qualities of each fruit is vastly different. The same is true for each of us and the fruit in our lives.

Now we come to the point in history where the door back to God reopens. As prophesied hundreds of years before, John the Baptist comes preaching a message of repentance, or turning away from sin and back towards God. Matthew 3:8 quotes John's message as this: "Produce fruit consistent with repentance...." Isn't it interesting that God uses the same item (fruit) that led to separation to describe the path to reconciliation?

So what does fruit of repentance look like? To answer that question, let's go back to the garden. Fresh appealing fruit hanging from a lush green tree and a desire to be like God caused humans to first rebel against God. This fruit of disobedience separated humans from their Maker and led to centuries of unrest. Fruit of disobedience can look like a lot of things: lying, stealing, or putting one's self before God. While disobedience can take many forms, it always puts our desires before God's commands.

The word *repentance* in the original language is often translated as "turn" or "return," implying a change in direction. True repentance is turning from wrongdoing and returning to God. So what does the fruit of repentance look like? It varies just like real fruits vary. Fruit of repentance is based on each individual and the sin(s) that require repentance. Repentance could take the form of a public apology or paying back what was taken. It could be changing with whom you spend your Friday nights with and in what activities you engage. It could be repairing broken relationships or kicking a bad habit. Some fruits of repentance are like papayas— fast to bear fruit. Other fruits of repentance are more like mangosteen and might take a lifetime of effort and change. Because nobody is perfect, bearing the fruit of repentance is a lifelong endeavor.

The first step of returning to God sounds fairly simple on paper but is challenging in practice. The Bible gives us plenty of examples of what true repentance looks like. Here are a few examples of a drastic change in direction as well as a failed act of repentance.

Man who murders Christians becomes a follower of Christ (Acts 9:1-9)

Perhaps one of the greatest conversion accounts in the Bible is that of a man named Saul (better known by his Greek name Paul). Raised as a Jewish leader, he takes it upon himself to persecute, imprison, and even kill anyone who goes against the Jewish Law. At first he does not recognize Christ as the fulfillment of the Law and instead sees Christ as opposition to the Law. On the way to zealously capture and persecute Christians, he encounters Jesus and is forever changed. The rest of Paul's life we see him preaching the good news of Christ, encouraging Christians, and training others to faithfully serve God. Paul's repentance bears amazing fruit during his life and beyond as we are still learning from the letters he wrote to various churches.

Thief returns stolen money with interest (Luke 19:1-9)

Tax collectors were notorious in ancient Judaism for overcharging people when they collected taxes and therefore were often despised. A rich tax collector named Zacchaeus hears Jesus is coming through town. In order to get a better view, Zacchaeus climbs a tree. Jesus notices him, calls him down from the tree, and says He wanted to stay at Zacchaeus' house. He obliges, and while Jesus is there, Zacchaeus makes a huge change in his behavior (repentance) by committing half of his possessions to the poor and promising to pay back fourfold anyone he cheated. His desire to follow Jesus trumps his desire to benefit himself financially.

Rich man returns to money instead of Jesus (Mark 10:17-22)

Changing habits and lifestyles are not easy, and there are many who are unwilling to surrender their lives completely to Christ when it comes right down to it. While Jesus was traveling, a rich young man meet Jesus. In great respect, he kneels before Jesus and asks what he needs to do to inherit eternal life. Jesus reminds him that he already knows the commandments, which the young man proudly says he had kept since his youth. This man has spent his life living how God commands. However, Jesus knows there is one thing standing in the way of a full surrender.

> *And Jesus, looking at him, loved him, and said to him, "You lack one thing: go, sell all that you have and give to the poor, and you will have treasure in Heaven; and come, follow Me." Disheartened by the saying, he went away sorrowful, for he had great possessions.*
> – Mark 10:21-22

Money itself is not the issue with this young man. The problem Jesus sees is that the man loves money more than he loves God. He is not willing to repent and change his allegiance from money to God. This is an example of someone who claims to love God and largely lives as such but fails to bear the fruit of repentance. Living a good life is not good enough. God demands complete surrender.

The phrase "fruit of repentance" implies there is a visible, tangible outcome —"a fruit"— from our turning back to God. What fruits of repentance have you demonstrated in your life or witnessed in others?

Prayer

Maker of heaven and earth, Lord, thank You for giving us fruit trees. It is refreshing to look at them and see not only that You provide good food for us, but You also teach us important lessons through them.

We all fall short everyday. Through Your Son, You offer a way back into Your grace. Help us fully surrender to You and allow our repentance to bear fruit that helps others in their search for You.

Lord, if there are obstacles or things that stand in the way between us and full surrender, please help us to see these clearly. Help remove the barriers so we can return to You and Your life-giving grace.

In Jesus' name,
Amen

1. Read the 3 accounts listed on page 101. What do you find interesting or notable?

_____

_____

_____

_____

2. What is repentance?

_____

_____

_____

3. Paul knows he has been forgiven of much. How does he describe himself in his letter to a young man named Timothy? (I Timothy 1:15)

_____

_____

_____

4. Is the tax collector told how to make things right with those he had wronged?

_____

_____

5. Money is an obstacle for the rich young man. What obstacles in your life stand between you and a full surrender to God?

_____

_____

_____

6. "Godly grief produces a repentance that leads to salvation..." (2 Corinthians 7:10). Are there things you need to repent of and turn back to God?

_____

_____

_____

_____

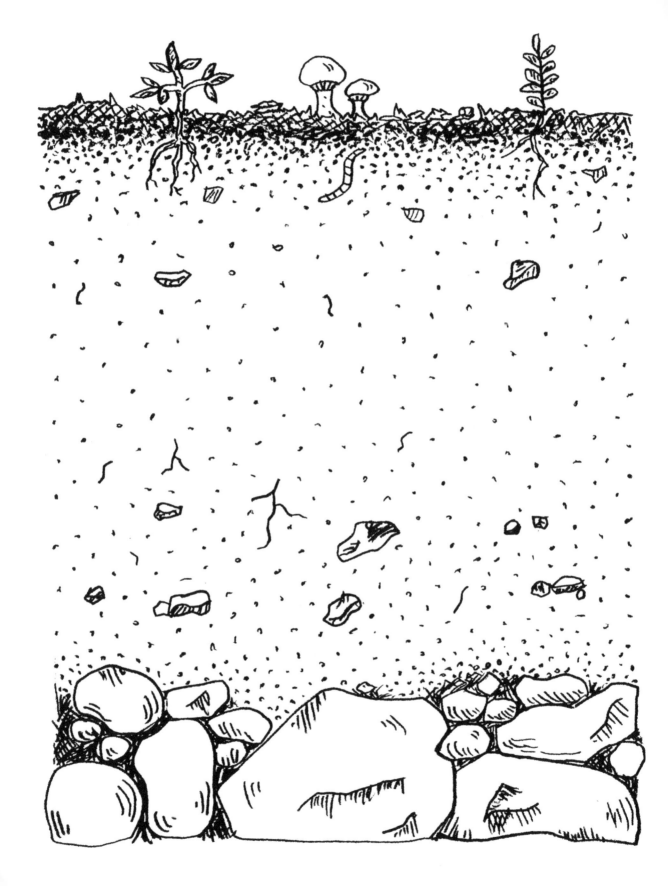

Good Soil

Did you know that the exact same grape seeds grown in the same region can mature and taste completely different based on the soil content and quality? Winemakers have discovered that grapes grown in aeolian soil (sandy soil that is transported by wind) mature faster and have a higher sugar content, higher-quality phenols, and produce a higher quality of wine than the grapes grown in silty soil.[24] *Terroir* (tĕr-wär) is the official word for this interesting phenomenon of soil playing a key role in how fruit grows and tastes, but it is not a new concept.

Jesus, who is traveling from place to place and teaching daily, shares a story that highlights the importance of good soil. In this parable (an earthly story with a spiritual meaning), a farmer sows seeds. The seeds are scattered on four different types of soil. The farmer gives every type of soil an equal opportunity to grow plants and bear fruit by spreading seeds on them all. It is the same type of seed that is scattered. The difference is the four distinct soil types where the seeds fall, which results in four very distinct outcomes.

1. Soil that falls on a path—the ground on the path is too packed down for the seeds to be buried, so the birds swoop down and eat the seeds before they have a chance to take root and grow.

2. Rocky ground—the seeds in rocky soil quickly spring up, but the rocks prevent them from developing deep roots. When the sun beats down these plants are quickly scorched. They cannot withstand heat or storms.

3. Soil with thorns—the seeds in soil plagued with thorny plants spring up but are choked out by the thorns as they start to grow.

4. Good soil—the seeds in the good soil spring up, the roots shoot down, and the seeds grow into thriving plants that later produce a bountiful harvest.

Jesus goes on to explain that the soil in this parable represents human hearts and the seed represents the Word of God. Just like the same grape seed can produce grapes with different qualities, the same truth of God's saving grace can produce different results based on the condition (the type of soil) of our hearts. As you read Luke 8:1-15, consider how the soil of your heart might be described.

In today's world, "thorny soil" that "chokes" the truth is such a challenge. What are these thorny life-taking plants? Anything that steals nutrients or prevents spiritual growth. It can be work stress or financial concerns. A toxic relationship or a harmful habit. Our hearts can be so busy consuming media or scrolling through social media that there is no space for God's good seed to grow. In fact, the "thorns" of media messages are growing at an incredibly alarming rate. In 2021, it was estimated the average person encountered up to 10,000 ads daily.[25] Ten thousand messages. Every. Single. Day. Our minds are reaching information overload before we have a chance to properly receive and tend to the life-giving message of God's saving love.

A second challenge to the information overload is the fact that the human brain needs to see, hear, or experience a message multiple times before buying in to the idea. Research varies on the exact number, but most agree the number is between three to seven exposures.[26] Businesses are hiring the best marketers they can afford and paying millions of dollars annually to ensure you are seeing their message frequently enough to spur you to action. Are we giving God's message the same amount of exposure in our lives? In Jesus' parable, the sower didn't plant just one seed in each type of soil but scattered them generously throughout. Not every seed of truth is going to be given the opportunity to take root and grow, so be sure to plant extra!

What if the soil of our hearts is already damaged or depleted? Is there no hope? Again, we go back to the knowledge of experienced gardeners and farmers. Skilled plant-whisperers can tell what is lacking in the soil by observing signs in the plants or relying on the accuracy of a soil test. Soil can be improved by adding the right nutrients, adjusting the pH, or planting the right type of crop. Our hearts, like a garden, can also be improved. We can make time in our busy lives to give God's Word a chance to take root. We can cut away the activities, places, or relationships that choke our spiritual growth. We can adjust our spiritual nutrient balance by spending more time in prayer and in God's Word and less time in messages from the world. When we find our hearts are not in the best shape, we can fix them with God's help!

So what exactly is the seed in this parable? It is the Word of God, the good news or the Gospel, that has the power to save if it is heard, believed, and put into practice. What exactly is the good news? One of the apostles summarizes the Gospel:

*Now I would remind you, brothers, of the Gospel I preached
to you, which you received, in which you stand, and by which
you are being saved, if you hold fast to the word I preached to
you—unless you believed in vain.*

*For I delivered to you as of first importance what I also received:
that Christ died for our sins in accordance with the Scriptures,
that He was buried, that He was raised on the third day in
accordance with the Scriptures, and that He appeared to
Cephas, then to the twelve.*

– 1 Corinthians 15:1-5

This good news is such good news. A lasting sacrifice has been made for us, which our sins require. Jesus died and was buried, but our hope didn't end there. Jesus rose from the dead and is now serving as the eternal King, as promised throughout Scripture. Allowing this "seed" to take root in our hearts leads us to turn away from evil, be "buried" with Christ in baptism, and rise out of the water as a new person with a new Spirit (God's Spirit) working in us and through us.

Prayer

Heavenly Father, thank You for providing seeds of truth in this world where so much is a lie. We are faced with so many distractions and temptations. Help us overcome the bad with the goodness that only comes from You!

Help prepare the soil of each of our hearts so that when Your truth is planted, it can freely grow into thriving, fruit-producing plants.

Through the millions of messages we are exposed to, help Yours be the message we truly hear and put into practice, for Your message is the only one with the promise of eternal life.

In Jesus' perfect name,
Amen

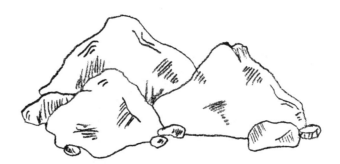

1. Read Luke 8:1-15. What do you find interesting or notable?

2. Who takes the seed of truth from hearts of those "along the path"? (Luke 8:12)

3. When do those with no roots fall away? (Luke 8:13)

4. What do the thorns do to the good seed? (Luke 8:14)

5. How would you honestly describe the soil of your own heart?

_____

_____

_____

_____

_____

_____

6. What can you immediately implement to improve the quality of your heart in order to be ready for the truth and bear better fruit?

_____

_____

_____

_____

_____

_____

_____

Palms for the King

Hollywood. If there is one thing the entertainment giant excels at, it is welcoming a celebrity. The red carpet gets rolled out. Crowds line up. Cheers erupt as the celebrities walk the red carpet.

The idea of laying out the red carpet is not a new one. In ancient Greek culture, red carpets were reserved for the gods of the time so they did not have to walk on the same ground mere mortals did. This tradition soon began to extend to royalty and highly esteemed leaders.

Jesus reaches this level of popularity by this point in His ministry. He has attracted the attention of the masses by performing miracles and teaching the wonders of God. Jesus heals the sick in the towns where He preaches. He casts out demons and raises the dead. He walks on water. He miraculously feeds over 5,000 people with a young boy's lunch. Even the Gentiles (the non-Jewish people) have taken note and realize this man is the Messiah (literally the "chosen one" in Hebrew and "Christ" in Greek) who had been foretold by the prophets of old. Jesus Himself verified he is the Messiah when He said He was one with God (John 10:30) and His Son (Mark 14:61-64). The people are ready to crown Jesus king.

Why crown Jesus a king? Well, the prophet Isaiah had predicted many years before Jesus was born that God's promise to Abraham, which was renewed through David, would result in a never-ending kingdom. In Isaiah 9:6-7 we read:

> *For a child will be born to us, a son will be given to us; And the government will rest on His shoulders; And His name will be called Wonderful Counselor, Mighty God, Eternal Father, Prince of Peace. There will be no end to the increase of His government or of peace, On the throne of David and over His kingdom, To establish it and to uphold it with justice and righteousness From then on and forevermore. The zeal of the Lord of hosts will accomplish this.*

However, the masses misunderstand this prophecy from God, as well as Jesus' own teaching. In Jeremiah 22:30, King Jehoachin (also known as Coniah) was punished for his evil ways. God Himself stated that no descendant of his would sit on the throne in Judah. In the genealogy of Jesus in Matthew 1:11, we see that indeed Jesus Christ is a descendant of Jehoachin, meaning that per God's decree, Jesus can not sit on an earthly throne in Judah. Jesus knows He is not meant to rule on earth. While standing trial, Jesus plainly proclaims, "My kingdom is not of this world" (John 18:36). Despite the clear messages God, Jesus, and the prophets of old, the crowds are so caught up in their excitement for an earthly king that they ignore these facts.

Jesus and the crowd approach Jerusalem where the people honor Him. As Jesus rides a donkey into the city, the people take their robes and throw them on the street and cover the street with palm leaves. This is their version of the red carpet treatment. The crowd begins to shout, praising God and exclaiming, "Blessed is the King who comes in the name of the Lord. Peace in heaven and glory in the highest!" (Luke 19:38). The people are ready for an earthly king, but God's plan is for Jesus' kingdom to be a heavenly one without end. Jesus has to evade the crowd's plan to make Him king by force (John 6:15).

So how do the people get the prophecies, God's decree, and Jesus' teaching so wrong? In psychology there is a term called confirmation bias. Confirmation bias is the tendency for people to favor information that confirms their existing beliefs or wishes. Evidence contrary to the established belief is often ignored or undervalued.[27] Confirmation bias tends to be stronger for deeply-rooted beliefs or emotional matters. The Jewish people had deeply entrenched beliefs that the Messiah would be an earthly king. They had been holding onto this hope for decade after decade. They sought evidence like Isaiah's prophecy that the "government will sit on His shoulders" to support an earthly reign (Isaiah 9:6) and tended to ignore Jesus' own teaching that contradicted their desire.

While the people celebrate the arrival of their long-awaited Messiah, the Jewish religious leaders grumble. Instead of seeing Jesus as the fulfillment of the prophecies, the Pharisees and Sadducees see Jesus as a threat to their power. They hate that Jesus sits with sinners and embraces the Gentiles (non-Jewish people). He even speaks against the hypocrisy of the Pharisees. Jesus represents everything the Jewish leaders fear: empowerment of the people, the end of the Jewish religious ruling class, and the passing away of the Old Law. The group that should be the first to see Jesus for who He is becomes the group that stands firmly opposed to His divinity and His life-giving message.

Hatred for Jesus and all that He represents grows among the Jewish religious leaders, and they desire to rid themselves of Jesus but fear the masses that follow Him. They continually look for a way to trap Jesus in His teaching so they can turn Him over to the governor. When this fails, the anger of the Jewish leaders leads them to look for a way to kill Jesus (Luke 22:2).

The long-awaited King and Messiah or an annoying threat to the highly prized status quo? Jesus was just as polarizing in His day as He is today. Who is Jesus to you?

Prayer

Oh King of Kings, ruler of all, Your power and might astound us. Your kingdom is unlike any the world has ever known. You rule with love instead of force. You welcome the unwelcomable. You grant mercy when punishment is deserved.

We read powerful accounts in the Bible of lives that were changed after coming in contact with You. Lord, as we come into contact with You through Your life-giving Word, transform our lives, heal our wounds, and cleanse our souls. Let our confession that You are Lord make us a part of Your never-ending kingdom.

In Jesus' merciful name,
Amen

1. Read Matthew 21:1-11. What do you find interesting or notable?

2. Why does Jesus send His disciples to find a donkey? (Matthew 21:1-5)

3. What do the crowds shout as Jesus rode into Jerusalem? (Matthew 21:9-10)

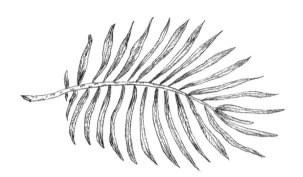

4. Who do the crowds say Jesus is? (Matthew 21:10-11)

5. Does Jesus embrace the idea of being a king on earth? (John 6:15 and John 18:36)

6. What deeply rooted beliefs (or confirmation bias) do you hold that may stand in the way of your recognizing the truth about Jesus?

The True Vine

Crowds are following Jesus in eager anticipation of an earthly king rising to power. The Jewish leaders are secretly looking for an opportunity to kill the Messiah. A traitor is quietly lurking in Jesus' inner circle. What sounds like the start of an adventure thriller is actually the intense reality of Jesus' life and ministry during His final days on earth.

Jesus knows hardships, betrayal, suffering and an excruciating death are quickly approaching, but instead of trying to escape it or avoid it, Jesus takes many opportunities to pull His followers in close and share messages of hope. He prepares His followers mentally for what is to come and gives them instructions on how to carry on in his absence.

With the whole world at His fingertips, Jesus once again uses plants to teach complex truths about God. In John 15, Jesus describes Himself as the vine and His father, God, as the vine dresser, the one who tenderly manages and cares for the vine. Humans are the branches in this metaphor.

So what does it mean that Jesus is the vine? Jesus is the living, life-giving source for the branches. Nutrients, stability, growth, and fruit all come from the vine. Branches that are part of the vine will thrive and bear fruit because the vine is richly providing everything the branches need. A branch that is cut off from the vine has been removed from its life source and is dead and useless. These dead, withered branches are thrown into the fire and destroyed while the fruit-bearing branches live on.

Farmers and gardeners know that even the highest quality of fruit-bearing plants require knowledgeable, consistent, and careful care. This is where God is the master gardener. God skillfully cares for and maintains the "true vine" of life. He prunes the branches that are not bearing fruit so that the vine overall can be more productive. We will later see that God also grafts branches into this life-giving vine.

The vine and the vine dresser are the constants, whereas the branches (every individual in the world) are the variables. Each one of us has a decision to make. Will we abide (remain) in the true vine (Jesus Christ) and faithfully bear fruit or will we be unfruitful, leading to us being cut-off from our life-giving source? Fruit or no fruit? Life or death? Jesus or the fire? God desires that you choose Him!

In John 15, Jesus continues to describe the amazing benefits of choosing a life in Christ. We see that those who abide (continually remain as one) in Christ will not only bear much fruit but will also be able to ask of God and He will hear! When we abide in Christ we are in God's love. And finally, the joy of the Lord will be in us and our joy may be full. In this world where there are struggles, pain, heartbreak, and uncertainty, what a promise to know that no matter what comes, our joy can be complete in Christ!

Up until this point in Jesus' ministry, Jesus was the teacher, and His followers, disciples (or learners). But in this passage, the relationship changes. Jesus offers His disciples the opportunity to shift from servants to friends! Think about that for a moment. The Son of God, who is ruler over all (1 Corinthians 15:27), is willing to call us His friends! On top of that, Jesus laid down His life once for all. All that is asked in return is for us to follow His commandments. In all measurements, it is an unbalanced friendship. Jesus paid the ultimate price and we are benefiting with a sense of belonging, life, love, and hope.

Have you ever considered the power of belonging? Most of us have experienced the heartache and pain that comes from being left out. Maybe it was being cut from a team or being excluded from the "in" group. Maybe the pain runs even deeper with being cut off from family. Humans, like many animals, were created to belong to a group.

God Himself noted that it is not good for man to be alone (Genesis 2:18). In *Tribes: We Need You to Lead Us*, author Seth Godin discusses the intrinsic desire humans have to belong to a group and the long history of tribal living. He explains how musicians, programmers, engineers, and business executives have succeeded, not because of their skills, but because they each built a tribe to which people were proud to belong.[28]

The rise of gang participation also provides us an example of the powerful urge to belong. What do gangs offer? In reality, individuals in a gang are more likely to die early, go to jail, or be involved in human trafficking.[29] However, gangs appeal to many insecure and vulnerable youth because they offer a sense of belonging (a "family" that will take care of them), protection, and a sense of purpose. The large number of people belonging to gangs underscores that the desire to belong often outweighs the risks.

God, who knows our innermost being (Psalm 139:13), knows full well our longing to belong. He places that yearning in our hearts! God strongly desires each one of us to choose to belong to Him. As Jesus teaches His followers, now called friends, those who channel their innate desire to belong to God will reap a plethora of rewards. Do you need more love, more joy, and more hope in your life?

Prayer

Dear God, though none of us have suffered like Jesus, we too struggle through opposition, betrayal, and crushed expectations. Instead of drawing in and giving up when challenges strike, help us to reach out with the hope that never disappoints.

Thank You for offering each of us the life-giving opportunity to be grafted into the True Vine, Your Son Jesus Christ. Help us to see Your hand in our lives as You tenderly care for each of us.

Despite all of life's challenges, we are so grateful that You fill us with Your joy. Help that joy to overflow from our hearts and bless others.

In the joyful name of Jesus,
Amen

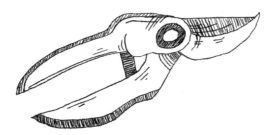

1. Read John 15:1-17. What do you find interesting or notable?

2. Why should we abide in Jesus? John 15:4-6)

3. What is the greatest example of love? (John 1:13)

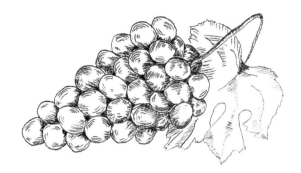

4. What requirement is there to be Jesus' friend? (John 1:14)

5. What are the requirements on our part when asking of God? (John 1:7, 17)

6. What can we learn about the nature of God as He is compared to a vine dresser?

Praying in the Garden

Have you ever kept devastating news quiet for a time? There are women who miscarry whose friends didn't even know about the pregnancy. There are managers who know layoffs are coming but don't have the liberty to share the news with their team. Or maybe there is a scary health diagnosis that won't be disclosed until further testing. Whatever the case, silently suffering even for a short time is downright hard.

Jesus knows full well the pain, betrayal, and ultimately the horrible death He will suffer. He tries to convey some of this to His closest friends and followers, but nobody really grasps the severity of it. Jesus is left carrying this devastating news largely alone. When it is too much for Jesus to bear, He takes His heavy heart to His Father—God.

Just as God met man in the garden, we see Jesus going to the garden to talk to God. This is not a one-time crisis call, but rather a habit (Luke 22:39). Troubling times are coming and Jesus specifically instructs His disciples to pray for strength to resist temptation. Jesus walks deeper into the garden and earnestly prays for a way out. He doesn't want to be betrayed by someone in his inner circle. He doesn't want to be whipped or insulted. He doesn't want to see the pain in His mother's eyes as He hangs on the cross. He doesn't want to die. Jesus is in such distress and praying so fervently, drops of sweat and blood run down His face. Jesus is at the end of the line, begging to be spared from the anguish He knows is coming, yet He doesn't run or hide from His purpose on Earth.

What Jesus says next is the reason we have hope today. In the midst of His sorrowful prayer, Jesus resolutely exclaims, "Nevertheless, not My will, but Yours, be done" (Luke 22:42). Think about that for a minute. The Son of God, who is declared ruler over all, makes a choice to powerfully submit to God's plan regardless of His own personal preference. Jesus endured more than most of us can even imagine because of His love for each one of us.

Jesus, who knows suffering is quickly approaching, could have chosen any activity that night to comfort, distract, or protect Himself. Why choose prayer? What power does prayer provide? Jesus makes a prayer a priority in His ministry and models how to pray. In Luke 11, Jesus teaches His disciples how to pray and make requests to God. Jesus assures His followers that just as an earthly father hears his children, our Heavenly Father (God) hears us. The Bible clearly states that God is not far from each one of us (Psalm 116:1). Our prayers are heard by God (Psalm 116:1) and answered by God (1 John 5:14-15). We are also assured that the prayers of the righteous are "powerful and effective" (James 5:16). Even more, God's Spirit intercedes for us when we can't find the right words (Romans 8:26). How comforting is that?!?

In addition, prayer appears to be a powerful antidote to worry and anxiety:

> *Do not be anxious about anything, but in everything by prayer and*
> *supplication with thanksgiving let your requests be made known to God.*
> *And the peace of God, which surpasses all understanding, will guard your*
> *hearts and your minds in Christ Jesus.*
> – Philippians 4:6-7

Science also verifies the positive power of prayer on our health and mental state. During the act of praying, the brain produces serotonin, which is a neurotransmitter that quells anxiety and creates a feeling of peace.[30] One study reported that individuals with strong religious beliefs and a habit of prayer were less anxious and depressed, had lower blood pressure, healed quicker, and demonstrated a stronger immune system.[31] Another study found regular prayer changes the physical structure of part of the brain's cortex, which is thought to guard against depression.[32] Prayer not only impacts our circumstances but it also changes us!

Strengthened by prayer and the angels ministering to Him, Jesus returns to His disciples, whom He left in prayer, only to find them asleep! Not just once, but twice Jesus returns to find His closest friends sleeping instead of joining Him in prayer (Matthew 26:36-46). What loneliness and frustration that must have caused. To make matters worse, it is at this moment that betrayal began in earnest. Judas, one of Jesus' apostles, the one His apostles trusted with the money, walks into the garden with a group armed with swords and clubs in the dark of night. Coming close to Jesus, he leans in and kisses his teacher, his mentor, the Son of God.

This kiss is not an act of respect or endearment, but rather the signal to the army indicating who they should arrest. Jesus refers to Judas' kiss of betrayal as the "power of the darkness," and dark indeed were the next few days.

The other disciples, now aware of what was going on, leap into action. Peter draws his sword, and in an effort to protect Jesus, cuts off the ear of the servant of the high priest. Jesus immediately calls for peace and shows extreme compassion for His enemies. In this high stress, emotionally tense moment of betrayal, Jesus sees fit to heal His enemy's ear. With no further opposition, Jesus is taken into custody in the dark of the night.

Prayer

Oh Father, "not My will but Yours...." What a powerful lesson Your Son teaches us in His darkest moment. We learn so much about true strength and the power of full submission to Your perfect will. Please grant us courage to stay focused on You and submit to Your will today and always.

Please help us forgive our friends when we lean on them and they let us down. Jesus did not banish His friends when they failed but instead offered grace. Help us to not hold grudges, but grant grace like Your Son models so beautifully for us.

In Jesus' name,
Amen

1. Read Luke 22:31-62. What do you find interesting or notable?

2. Jesus' friends fail Him by falling asleep. How does He respond? (Luke 22:40-47)

3. With what is Jesus betrayed? (Luke 22:47-49)

4. With what attitude does Jesus approach His enemies? (Luke 22:47-54)

5. Jesus knew Peter would fail. What does He instruct Peter to do immediately after "turning back" or repenting? (Luke 22:31-32)

6. In what ways or in what venues do you find yourself regularly denying Jesus?

Hung on a Tree

"If I tell you, you won't believe it." Many incredulous tales have been recounted following an introduction like this. True accounts that seem implausible are more likely to instill doubt rather than belief in the information presented. In fact, human beings are wired just as much for denial as we are for belief. So how can humans who are gifted with high level cognitive abilities ignore facts? The answer is tied to the intense emotions that human beings experience. Psychologists acknowledge our emotions and preconceived notions often overshadow the actual evidence of a situation, and changing preexisting ideologies requires more than just facts.[33] This is one reason that the captivating, historically-documented life, death, and resurrection of Jesus Christ has been met with disbelief from then until now.

Truly considering Jesus and His teachings is uncomfortable. It requires us to see ourselves in an unattractive and powerless manner: sinners in need of a Savior. But as psychologists warn, denial of truth can be dangerous.[34] Today, look at the account of Jesus from a fresh perspective. Bravely let down your guard and embrace the discomfort of personal imperfection. Allow the incredible, hard-to-believe, proven account of Jesus Christ, the Son of the Almighty God, to radically transform your life.

After Jesus was taken into custody, the time comes for Him to stand before His accusers so a judgment can be made about the charges levied against Him. Standing before the council, Jesus is plainly asked, "If You are the Christ, tell us" (Luke 22:67). Jesus knowingly reasons, "If I tell you, you will not believe" (Luke 22:68). Then Jesus continues sharing a truly incredulous image of His future: sitting at the right hand of God. In this passage and the verses that follow, Jesus makes claims that to this day some still struggle to believe. Jesus reveals Himself to be the Christ, the Son of God, and the King of the Jews. Those opposed to Jesus use these claims to find Him guilty of blasphemy (Matthew 26:64-65). They misconstrue Jesus' teaching and falsely accuse Him of misleading a nation, undermining political authority, claiming power as a king, stirring people up, and claiming deity. Now Jesus—betrayed, arrested, mocked, and abandoned is being called to defend Himself.

Jesus is brought before Pontius Pilate, a Roman governor documented in historical accounts in addition to the Bible.[35] Pilate questions Jesus and firmly indicates that he finds no guilt in Jesus. The anger of the crowd is not satisfied, and they persist in their accusations. Once Pilate hears Jesus is from Galilee, he sends Jesus to Herod who ruled over Galilee.[36] Herod, who had heard about the miracles and signs of Jesus, hoped to witness Jesus' mighty works in person. Herod questions Jesus, but Jesus gives no answers despite the angry accusations that are continuing to be hurled. Herod mocks Jesus, dresses Him in kingly garments, and sends Him back to Pilate. For the second time Pilate reiterates that he finds no guilt in Jesus that deserves death and announces he will punish and release Jesus. The crowd does not relent and continues shouting, "Crucify!" Pilate, wanting to release Jesus, again proclaims, "What evil has He done?" (Luke 23:22). The crowd ignores Pilate and urgently demands that Jesus be crucified. Pilate allows their angry voices to prevail. Sadly, sometimes the loudest voices triumph over justice. In order to appease the crowd, Pilate delivers an innocent man into their hands to be killed on a cross.

In mockery, a crown of thorns is thrust on Jesus' head as He is nailed to the cross. A sign that reads "King of the Jews" is placed over His head. Despite the unjust and brutal treatment, Jesus, full of mercy, offers forgiveness to all. Darkness engulfs the land even though it is still day. Jesus commits His Spirit to God and takes His last labored breath. The innocent Lamb of God is dead. Jesus is buried in a cave tomb and a huge boulder is rolled in front of it, sealing it off. Soldiers are commanded to guard the grave to ensure Jesus' body is not stolen.

If the account ends here, all hope is lost. Praise God there is more to the story! Just as the prophets and Jesus foretold, death is not victorious. After the Sabbath (a Jewish day of rest) the women return to the grave and find a truly remarkable site. The stone has been rolled away, and where Jesus' body once laid are two dazzling figures who joyfully announce Jesus is not dead, but alive. He has risen!

The idea of rising from the dead goes against the very grain of the fallen world we live in, and it can be genuinely hard to believe. Thankfully, God doesn't require blind faith. He provides evidence to help us accept this truly amazing phenomenon that serves as the very core of our hope and salvation. Following the women's viewing of the empty tomb, Jesus Christ appears to many in human form (1 Corinthians 15:6).

His disciples are able to physically touch the wounds in Jesus' hands and feet and witness Jesus eating food—things that would not be possible for a spirit or a ghost (Luke 24: 39). The resurrection also gave courage to the fearful disciples who come out of hiding and start proclaiming the amazing news that our Savior has risen. Jesus also appears to His half brother James, who before the resurrection was skeptical of Jesus' claims. After seeing his brother Jesus risen from the dead, James becomes a courageous and outspoken leader in the church.

During the days after Jesus' resurrection, He spends time connecting all the dots through Scripture. Jesus begins with Moses and the Prophets and explains how He is the fulfillment to all that has been written concerning the Messiah. Jesus opens His apostles' minds so they can fully understand all that had been previously written (Luke 24:45). Now that Jesus' work is fully completed on earth, He blesses His disciples and is taken up into Heaven right before their eyes!

Wow. The life, death, and resurrection of Jesus Christ is a lot to take in. Jesus' apostle John tells us the world could not contain records of all that Jesus did while He was here on Earth (John 21:25), but these things were recorded "so that you may believe that Jesus is the Christ, the Son of God, and that by believing you may have life in His name" (John 20:30-31). The account that starts with "You won't believe it…" ends with "So that you may believe." Belief in Jesus our Savior leads to obedience and life in His name.

Prayer

Wonderful Father, grant us open minds and humble hearts as we read this amazing account of Your Son. Help us overcome denial. Open our eyes to the truth.

We are so grateful that Jesus was willing to take our sins to that terrible tree. We are touched that He was willing to die for us, despite our constant shortcomings and mistakes. From the first sin in the garden, a sacrifice was required for sin, and You sent Your Son to be this blameless sacrifice once and for all.

Jesus left the earth, but not without first equipping us. Thank You for sending Your Spirit, giving us the truth, and above all else, for loving us so deeply.

In Jesus' saving name,
Amen

1. Read Luke 22:63–24:12, What do you find interesting or notable?

2. Do the governors Pilate and Herod find any guilt in Jesus? (Luke 23:13-16)

3. How would you describe Jesus' crucifixion? (Luke 23:44-49)

4. What proof of His resurrection does Jesus offer His followers? (Luke 24:1-12)

5. How do His followers come to understand that Jesus fulfills Scripture? (Luke 24:-27)

6. What part of this account is most challenging for you to believe? Why?

Grafted In

In the middle of the Pacific Ocean on the island of Oahu, there is a lush tree farm planted in a valley of the Ko'olau Mountains. Frankie's Nursery is known far and wide for their high quality fruit trees that bear hundreds of varieties of tropical fruit. Of particular interest is their prized avocado tree that grows 12 different types of avocados all on the same tree, each bearing fruit in its own season. How is this even possible? Through a process called grafting, branches from one variety can be attached onto a tree of a different variety. The newly grafted branches will bear the variety of fruit from the tree from which it came.[37] To create this amazing tree, the skilled farmers at Frankie's Nursery grafted in branches from 12 different avocado varieties. The original tree supplies the nutrients through its roots while the branches each bear the grafted variety of fruit.

We see this same idea of grafting in the Bible. Recall the original promise God made Abraham that was renewed through David. God's chosen people (the Jews) were to be blessed. Over time, this special designation led to poor treatment of non-Jewish people. In fact, the Jews' racism became so intense at one point that Jews would not even speak to non-Jewish people. Jesus, the champion of love, refused to succumb to treating any group or culture poorly.

The Jews are shocked to see Jesus eating and drinking with "sinners"—another name given to the Gentiles who didn't serve God (Luke 15:1-7). Even Jesus' closest followers who heard Jesus' teachings firsthand are surprised to see Him talking with a Samaritan woman (John 4:27). Jesus introduces a new code of conduct for believers; however, it takes some time for His followers to reverse their deeply held stereotypes.

When we looked at the parable of the vine back in Chapter 15, we saw how Jesus is described as the true vine. After Jesus' death, one of His apostles Paul, uses a similar metaphor to explain how God's promise is not just for the Jews, but a promise of full inclusion to all people.

In Romans 11:17, Paul explains some of the "natural" branches (Jews) were broken off due to unbelief and "wild olive shoots" (non-Jews or Gentiles) were grafted in and can now share in the nourishing root of the olive tree (Jesus Christ). Peter, another apostle, speaks a similar message to the Jews the first time the Gospel (the good news of Jesus Christ) is shared after Jesus' death and resurrection.

> *Repent and be baptized every one of you in the name of Jesus Christ for the forgiveness of your sins, and you will receive the gift of the Holy Spirit. For the promise is for you and for your children and for all who are far off, everyone whom the Lord our God calls to Himself.*
> – Acts 2:38-39

Though he is speaking to the Jews, Peter is clear that the promise is to the Jews and to those who are "far off" (non-Jews). Everyone. God is not a God of discrimination. What an amazing promise that we can hold on to in this world that is full of racism, division, and lack of inclusion. God calls each one of us to be grafted into His life-giving tree.

In the farming world, only the best varieties are chosen for grafting. Thanks be to God we are all invited, from the least of us to the greatest to be added to the life-giving tree of Jesus Christ. How? As Peter shares shortly after Jesus' death, we need to believe that Jesus is God's Son and turn away from sin and turn back towards God (repentance). Once hearts and minds are firmly pointed and committed to Jesus, baptism follows. The original Hebrew word that has been translated into baptism literally means to immerse. Baptism is a symbolic washing away of our sins (1 Peter 3:21) and a symbolic burial with Jesus (Romans 6:3, 4, 5; Colossians 2:12). Through baptism, we receive the gift of the Holy Spirit, which is the Spirit of God Himself (Ephesians 4:4-6)! He lives in and works through us, guides us, comforts us, and gives us hope (John 14:26; 1 Corinthians 2:12-13; Romans 15:13). What a truly amazing gift!

Since Jesus already paid the price for our sins, simply acknowledging Jesus as God's Son, turning towards Him, putting our sinful selves to "death" and "rising" as a new creation through baptism will allow us to become children of God (Galatians 2:20). Like Jesus, we will one day overcome death and live forever with God in Heaven (1 Thessalonians 4:14). Until then, we live on earth by the Spirit bearing good fruit (Galatians 5:22-23), which we'll talk about in more detail in the next chapter. It is important to note that the promise of life eternal is conditional. Romans 11:22-23 explains the kindness of God is granted to those who continue in Him. If we stop bearing the fruit of repentance and obedience, Romans explains we will be cut off as a farmer cuts off branches that don't produce good fruit.

Grace and mercy are abundantly poured out to those who seek it. However, this unmatchable kindness comes from God who has also promised to deal severely with those who refuse the precious gift of life. God holds in His hands two polar opposites: life and death. Matthew 7:19 warns that trees who do not bear good fruit are cut down and thrown into the fire. Grafted in or cut off. Reward or suffering. Comfort or agony. Kindness or severity. Each of us gets to make the choice for ourselves. God greatly desires that each of us seek Him:

> *For God so loved the world, that He gave His only Son, that whoever*
> *believes in Him should not perish but have eternal life. For God did not*
> *send His Son into the world to condemn the world, but in order that the*
> *world might be saved through Him.*
>
> – John 3:16-17

Prayer

To the God of us all, thank You for creating all people with such a beautiful tapestry of ethnicities and cultures. Though You made Yourself known through a chosen people for a time, You demonstrated over and over again, that You are the God of inclusion. It doesn't matter if we are Jew or Gentile, Your promise extends to us all and to everyone who calls on Your name.

As kind as Your promise is, we recognize there is a severity to it as well. Life is granted for living a life of obedience, but death is the reality for those who choose not to be grafted into the true vine. Lord, soften the soil of our hearts so we can be receptive to Your offer.

In Jesus' life-giving name,
Amen

1. Read Romans 11:11-24. What do you find interesting or notable?

2. What attitude should we have about our inclusion in the promise? (Romans 11:20)

3. Once removed, can a branch be grafted back in? (Romans 11:23)

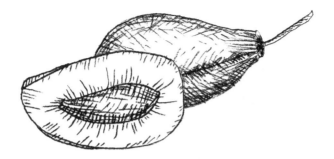

4. What did the Jews' jealousy accomplish? (Romans 11:14-16)

5. What steps do we need to take to be "grafted" in? (Acts 2:38-39)

6. How would you describe the "kindness" and "severity" of God? (Romans 11:22)

Fruit of the Spirit

There are some who can walk up to a tree and immediately know what kind it is by the shape of its leaves, but for most of us, not until there are big, ripe, juicy oranges hanging from branches do we know for certain we are looking at an orange tree. Most fruits are so distinct in their appearance there is no confusing an apple with a peach or a lime with a lemon. The Bible tells us we should be producing fruit in our own lives that is clearly recognized as fruit of the Spirit, not fruit of the flesh.

> *The fruit of the Spirit is love, joy, peace, patience, kindness, goodness,*
> *faithfulness, gentleness, self-control.*
> – Galatians 5:22-24

Our lives are ripe with opportunities to grow such beautiful fruit that will undoubtedly attract others to us, and ultimately to Christ. Each of these fruits are discussed in detail throughout the Bible, and studying each one allows us to better cultivate them in our own lives. Of all of these fruits, there are two that are often neglected or severely misunderstood: love and self-control. Love, according to *Merriam Webster*, is either a noun meaning "a strong feeling of attraction or affection" or a transitive verb "to hold dear or cherish."[38] In both instances, and in most of the world's use of the word *love*, it has to do with a fleeting feeling of attraction. We hear of people "falling in love" or "falling out of love" as if the feeling of love either captivates or escapes you. This is not the kind of love to which the Bible is referring.

Agape is the type of love mentioned in this passage. *Agape* love is the highest form of unconditional love and is further defined in 1 Corinthians 13:4-8. In this passage, love is not portrayed as a feeling but rather an action verb. The magnitude of what love is goes even further when we read that God is love (1 John 4:8). Understanding that the first fruit of the Spirit reflects the very nature of God emphasizes the importance of cultivating love in our own lives.

Then we come to self-control, the forgotten fruit. In *Willpower: Rediscovering the Greatest Human Strength*, the authors cite a recent survey of over one million people who ranked self-control last when asked about their personal strengths and first when asked about what traits they struggle with. Authors Roy Baumeister and John Tierney concluded that "self-regulation (self-control) is the major pathology of our time."[39] That is a pretty powerful claim, but divorce rates, domestic violence trends, crime statistics, and obesity all support the idea that lack of self-control is wreaking havoc on our lives. Perhaps that is why this fruit is listed as the culmination of the fruits of the Spirit. Without self-control, it is impossible to consistently choose joy or to remain patient in the face of ongoing pressure. It takes a great deal of self-control to be kind to those who mistreat you or to remain steadfast in peaceful efforts when those around you are warring. It is hard to be full of faith in a world full of doubt.

God requires self-control from His people, and psychologists have given us a glimpse of why self-control is such a powerful trait to possess and further cultivate. Individuals with high levels of self-control:

- Are more successful at maintaining relationships
- Empathize more effectively with others
- Tend to be less anxious or depressed
- Harbor less anger and aggression
- Boast of better health
- Enjoy greater financial stability
- Suffer less divorce

The researchers conclude, "Self-control is a vital strength in life." Both science and Scripture validate the importance of self-control, but how do we better cultivate that fruit in our own lives? Thankfully there are many ways to build our self-control muscle. In *Willpower: Rediscovering the Greatest Human Strength*, the authors provide many tried and true methods for increasing our self-control and avoiding the pitfalls of temptation:

- Maintain an orderly living environment. Humans make better choices in cleaner spaces.
- "Set your mind on things above" as Colossians 3:2 tells us. Focusing on high level thoughts, life's purpose, and long-term goals increase willpower.
- Keep your image in mind. When participants could see themselves in a mirror, they were more likely to stay true to their inner values, act less aggressively, and behave more honestly.

- Establish strong habits that set you up for success instead of habits like procrastination that require a last ditch effort to succeed.
- Take care of your body with healthy food, exercise, and good sleep.
- Keep track of your successes and failures and reward the good.[39]

God calls us to continually increase self-control and add it to the other fruits of the Spirit. Not only will this benefit our everyday relationships and activities, but the Bible promises that increasing self-control keeps us from being ineffective and unproductive in our knowledge of Jesus (2 Peter 1:8).

God has graciously given us everything we need to live through His Son Jesus and bear the life-giving fruit of the Spirit. Not only do we honor God and bless others by doing so, but God also promises we will be rewarded with a harvest of righteousness.

> But the wisdom from above is first pure, then peaceable, gentle, open to reason, full of mercy and good fruits, impartial and sincere. And a harvest of righteousness is sown in peace by those who make peace.
> – James 3:17-18

Prayer

Mighty God, thank You for giving us everything we need for life and godliness. You have given us a glimpse of the benefits of bearing good fruit and we desire to do so. Give us strength to overcome the desires of the flesh so we can be filled with Your Spirit.

Help us as we seek to increase and strengthen our love, joy, peace, patience, kindness, goodness, faithfulness, gentleness, and our self-control. May others be drawn to You by the fruit we bear.

In Jesus' name,
Amen

1. Read Galatians 5:16-26. What do you find interesting or notable?

2. How does this passage describe the desires of the flesh? (Galatians 5:16-22)

3. What are the fruits of the Spirit? (Galatians 5:22-24)

4. How is love described in 1 Corinthians 13:4-8?

_____

_____

_____

5. Why should we continue to increase in the fruits of the Spirit? (2 Peter 1:3-11)

_____

_____

_____

6. How have those in Christ "crucified the flesh with its passions and desires?" (Galatians 5:24. See also Galatians 2:20.)

_____

_____

_____

The Tree of Life

Another year. Another ring. Another candle. Both trees and humans mark each incredible trip around the sun. The years fly by and we have a tangible reminder of time. In the physical world, there is a clear beginning and end. A tree starts as a seed, and when it dies the rings around the trunk stop multiplying. Humans enter the world through the amazing process of birth and leave the world in the often dreaded exit of death. Then what? Those in Christ are raised new into a breathtaking place that is being prepared for us where life is everlasting. It can be hard to wrap our human minds around the idea of life without end, though our souls are instinctively wired for it. Solomon in Ecclesiastes 3:11 explains that God put eternity into our hearts which explains why fear of dying is consistently ranked one of the top fears.[40] One day, time as we know it will end, and humans will be reconciled to their Maker. When? The day and the hour are only known to God (Mark 13:32).

Eternity begins with the return of Jesus. After Jesus ascended into Heaven, His disciples were staring at the sky in wonder and amazement. An angel asks them, "Men of Galilee, why do you stand looking into heaven? This Jesus, who was taken up from you into Heaven, will come in the same way as you saw Him go into Heaven" (Acts 1:1). We are told that in a twinkling of an eye, trumpets will sound, the dead will rise, and we will be changed from mortal bodies to immortal ones (1 Corinthians 15:50-55). What an incredible mental picture! What will eternity be like?

Eternity will be a restoration of how life was intended: humans with their Maker. The apostle John was given a sneak-peak of Heaven through a vision. In his words:

> *And I heard a loud voice from the throne saying, "Behold, the dwelling place of God is with man. He will dwell with them, and they will be His people, and God Himself will be with them as their God. He will wipe away every tear from their eyes, and death shall be no more, neither shall there be mourning, nor crying, nor pain anymore, for the former things have passed away."*
> – Revelation 21:3-4

Just like God walked with Adam and Eve in the Garden of Eden, those in Christ can eagerly anticipate walking with the Maker in the breathtaking beauty of Heaven.

Eternity will be healing.
As physical trees bring healing in this life, the Tree of Life provides spiritual healing in the next.[41] Through the curse resulting from sin in the Garden of Eden (Genesis 3:16-19), access to this tree was removed, but those in Christ are free from the curse through Jesus (Revelation 22:3) and will have access to this tree once again (Revelation 22:14). As Romans 5:12-21 explains, disobedience and death entered the world through one man Adam, obedience and life also entered through one man Jesus Christ.

John continues to share his vision of Heaven in Revelation 22:1-2:

> *Then the angel showed me the river of the water of life, bright as crystal,*
> *flowing from the throne of God and of the Lamb through the middle of the*
> *street of the city; also, on either side of the river, the Tree of Life with its*
> *twelve kinds of fruit, yielding its fruit each month. The leaves of the tree*
> *were for the healing of the nations.*

In Heaven, our pain, our hurts, and our tears will all be washed away. Constant provision will be provided. Our bodies and our souls will experience a level of healing that we should all eagerly anticipate!

Eternity is an unsurpassed reward for those in Christ.

Have you ever imagined what it would be like to be royalty? To have the privileges and honor that comes with the title? As children of the true King, those in Heaven will be rewarded with the "unfading crown of glory" (1 Peter 5:4). While this amazing gift is offered for all, each individual must personally make a choice: Will I obey God and enter eternal life through His Son Jesus Christ, or will I ignore the opportunity of this life and next? The only way to Heaven is through Jesus, who is the way, the truth, and the life (John 14:16). Will your life bear the spiritual fruit of obedience to God or will busyness, selfishness, or poor heart soil lead to the fruit of disobedience? What seeds do you plant and cultivate in your day-to-day life?

> *For the one who sows to his own flesh will from the flesh reap corruption,*
> *but the one who sows to the Spirit will from the Spirit reap eternal life.*
> – Galatians 6:8

Reward or punishment. We get to choose! Sharing eternal life with Jesus requires sharing in death by putting our selfish selves to death and being buried in the waters of baptism. John describes this process as "washing robes" in Revelation 22:14:

> *Blessed are those who wash their robes, so that they may have the right to the Tree of Life and that they may enter the city by the gates.*

Can you imagine seeing the Tree of Life and being offered its healing and life-giving fruit? Heaven is almost unfathomable and yet at the same time at our fingertips!

So what does this mean for you and me? Knowing our ultimate desired destination should determine the path we take today and every day. As Steven Covey notes in his book *The 7 Habits of Highly Effective People*, beginning with the end in mind leads to greater success in achieving a goal than simply setting off in any given direction.[42] If Heaven is truly your ultimate destination, then what adjustments do you need to make in your life in order to stay on course?

As our study comes to an end, meditate and pray on that question. Your very life depends on the decision you make today. Tomorrow is not promised. Life on this earth is fragile and fast (James 4:13-24). Put your trust in the unfailing promises of God. It is in God and Christ Jesus where hope grows free.

Prayer

Oh Lord, You are the beginning and the end. Through Your deep and merciful love, You provide a way back to the Tree of Life, a way back to You! There is no better culmination to life on earth than entering a peaceful, joyful, healing, everlasting rest and reward.

With that end in mind, oh Lord, please guide our steps, our minds, and our hearts in the world today. Remove any seeds of doubt and bitterness and nourish the seed of truth that is now planted in each of our hearts. May this seed of truth grow into a vibrant, life-giving tree, saving our souls and bringing hope to those in our circles of influence.

In Jesus' saving name,
Amen

1. Read Revelation 22. What do you find interesting or notable?

2. Are we to worship any other spiritual being? (Revelation 22:8-9)

3. Who will be left outside the gates of Heaven? (Revelation 22:15)

4. Who does Jesus say He is? (Revelation 22:16)

_____

_____

_____

5. What invitation does the Spirit and the Bride (the church) offer? (Revelation 22:17)

_____

_____

6. What aspect(s) of Heaven do you look forward to the most?

_____

_____

_____

The seed has now been
planted in your heart.

May it take root and
save your soul.

Acknowledgments

Therefore, since we are surrounded by so great a cloud of witnesses, let us also lay aside every weight, and sin which clings so closely, and let us run with endurance the race that is set before us, looking to Jesus, the founder and perfecter of our faith, who for the joy that was set before him endured the cross, despising the shame, and is seated at the right hand of the throne of God.
– Hebrews 12:1-2

I am so blessed to have been surrounded by so many amazing witnesses of God's love. While there are too many to thank adequately in this space, this book is in your hands today due to the love and support of:

Sharon Laidler, my dear aunt and a life-long teacher, who spent countless hours offering encouragement and suggestions. **Cheryl Alt**, my mom and #1 supporter, used her spelling bee championship skills to wade through my misspellings just like when I was a kid! **Andrew Arbuckle**, my husband, shared powerful links between topics. **Eva, Alana, and Oralee Arbuckle**, my daughters, cheered me on and reminded me to gracefully embrace the beauty and naturalness of imperfection. **Ramani Bickel** taught me so much about fruit trees. I hope I accurately represented her favorite fruits through the illustrations! **Steve Byrne**, an amazing spiritual thinker, carefully reviewed my first draft. **Tracy Graham**, through her quiet strength and solid dedication, has taught me so much. **Verna Enfinger**, a loyal friend, supported me in many ways. **Heather Jones**, thank you for encouraging me to start this amazing journey! Last, but not least, thank you to the entire hardworking team at **Kaio Publications** who played an integral role in transforming an idea into a beautiful, finished product. To the rest of **my village**, I love you all!

Notes

Chapter 1: The World's First Garden

1. Li, Qing. *Forest Bathing: How Trees Can Help You Find Health and Happiness*. Viking, 2018.
2. Kühn, Simone, et al. "In Search of Features That Constitute an 'Enriched Environment' in Humans: Associations between Geographical Properties and Brain Structure." *Nature News*, Nature Publishing Group, 20 Sept. 2017, https://www.nature.com/articles/s41598-017-12046-7.
3. Michigan State University. "Playing Outside Could Make Kids More Spiritual." *ScienceDaily*, 1 May 2014, http://www.sciencedaily.com/releases/2014/05/140501101137.htm.

Chapter 2: A Single Olive Branch

4. The Arbinger Institute. *The Anatomy of Peace - Resolving the Heart of Conflict*. Berrett-Koehler Publishers, 2006.

Chapter 3: Under the Oak Grove

5. Doebel, S, et al. "Good Things Come to Those Who Wait: Delaying Gratification Likely Does ..." *Psychological Science*, 18 Dec. 2019, https://journals.sagepub.com/doi/10.1177/0956797619839045.

Chapter 4: Caught in the Thicket

6. Guy-Evans, Olivia. "Amygdala Hijack and the Fight or Flight Response." *Simply Psychology*, 16 June 2021, http://www.simplypsychology.org/what-happens-during-an-amygdala-hijack.html.

Chapter 5: When There Is No Harvest

7. Castrillon, Caroline. "5 Ways To Go From a Scarcity to Abundance Mindset." *Forbes*, Forbes Magazine, 12 Oct. 2022, http://www.forbes.com/sites/carolinecastrillon/2020/07/12/5-ways-to-go-from-a-scarcity-to-abundance-mindset/?sh=498c22731197.

Chapter 6: Hope from the Bulrushes

8. Gillett, Tracy. "Everything You Need to Know About Secure Attachment." *Raised Good*, 27 May 2021, https://raisedgood.com/everything-you-need-to-know-about-secure-attachment/.

Chapter 7: Orchards You Didn't Plant

9. Mcleod, Saul. "Solomon Asch - Conformity Experiment." *Simply Psychology*, 28 Dec. 2018, http://www.simplypsychology.org/asch-conformity.html.

Chapter 8: Trees Planted By Streams of Water

10. Buckingham, M. "What Really Makes Us Resilient?" *Harvard Business Review*, 30 Aug. 2021, https://hbr.org/2020/09/what-really-makes-us-resilient.
11. Walsh, Erin. "Building Resilience: Your Family Stories Matter." *Spark & Stitch Institute*, 9 Apr. 2020, https://sparkandstitchinstitute.com/building-resilience-family-stories/.

12. Burnett, John. "After Hurricane's Wrath, Puerto Rico's Green Forests Turn Bare Brown." NPR, 1 Oct. 2017, http://www.npr.org/2017/10/01/554753135/after-hurricane-s-wrath-puerto-rico-s-green-forests-turn-bare-brown.

Chapter 9: Wisdom From the Trees

13. "The Pygmalion Effect." *The Decision Lab*, https://thedecisionlab.com/biases/the-pygmalion-effect.

Chapter 10: A Root out of Dry Ground

14. Boghani, P. "How Poverty Can Follow Children into Adulthood." *PBS*, 22 Nov. 2017, http://www.pbs.org/wgbh/frontline/article/how-poverty-can-follow-children-into-adulthood/.
15. Henderson, Anne T., and Karen L. Mapp. "A New Wave of Evidence: The Impact of School, Family, and Community Connections on Student Achievement." *ERIC*, 30 Nov. 2001, https://eric.ed.gov/?id=ED474521.
16. Stoner, Peter Winebrenner, and Robert C. Newman. *Science Speaks: Scientific Proof of the Accuracy of Prophecy and the Bible*. Online ed., Moody Press, 2005.

Chapter 11: A Gnarled Family Tree

17. Paul, Ian. "Jesus Wasn't Born in a Stable- And That Makes All the Difference." *Psephizo*, 30 Nov. 2020, http://www.psephizo.com/biblical-studies/jesus-wasnt-born-in-a-stable-and-that-makes-all-the-difference.
18. Chaffey, Tim. "Born in a Barn (Stable)?" *Answers in Genesis*, 21 Dec. 2020, https://answersingenesis.org/christmas/born-in-a-barn-stable/.
19. "Eyewitness Identification Reform." *Innocence Project*, 17 Dec. 2020, https://innocenceproject.org/eyewitness-identification-reform/.

Chapter 12: Fruit of Repentance

20. M., Aniela. "How to Grow Papaya from Seed." *Plant Instructions*, 15 Mar. 2017, https://plantinstructions.com/tropical-fruit/grow-papaya-seed/.
21. Taylor, Craig. "Growing Mangosteen: How to Plant, Raise and Harvest the Queen of Tropical Fruit." *Morning Chores*, 20 Aug. 2021, https://morningchores.com/growing-mangosteen/.
22. Jahangir, Abbas. "Jackfruit: The World's Largest Fruit!" *Foods Trend*, 5 Sept. 2021, https://foodstrend.com/jackfruit/.
23. Jennings, Kerri-Ann. "Durian Fruit: Smelly but Incredibly Nutritious." *Healthline*, 31 May 2019, http://www.healthline.com/nutrition/durian-fruit.

Chapter 13: Good Soil

24. Wang, Rui, et al. "Soil Types Effect on Grape and Wine Composition in Helan Mountain Area of Ningxia." *PLOS ONE*, Public Library of Science, 23 Feb. 2015, https://journals.plos.org/plosone/article?id=10.1371%2Fjournal.pone.0116690.
25. Carr, Sam. "How Many Ads Do We See a Day in 2023?" *Lunio*, 19 Jan. 2023, https://lunio.ai/blog/strategy/how-many-ads-do-we-see-a-day/.
26. Kruse, Kathi. "Rule of 7: How Social Media Crushes Old School Marketing." *Kruse Control Inc*, 14 Aug. 2022, http://www.krusecontrolinc.com/rule-of-7-how-social-media-crushes-old-school-marketing-2021/.

Chapter 14: Palms for the King

27. Noor, Iqra. "How Confirmation Bias Works." *Simply Psychology*, 10 June 2020, http://www.simplypsychology.org/confirmation-bias.html.

Chapter 15: The True Vine

28. Godin, Seth. *Tribes: We Need You To Lead Us.* Penguin, 2008.
29. Lohmann, Raychelle C. "Teen Gangstas." *Psychology Today*, 11 Oct. 2010, https://www.psychologytoday.com/us/blog/teen-angst/201010/teen-gangstas.

Chapter 16: Praying in the Garden

30. Davis, Shirley. "The Mental Health Benefits of Prayer." *CPTSD Foundation*, 20 Jan. 2020, https://cptsdfoundation.org/2020/01/20/the-mental-health-benefits-of-prayer/.
31. Andrade, Chittaranjan, and Rajiv Radhakrishnan. "Prayer and Healing: A Medical and Scientific Perspective on Randomized Controlled Trials." *Indian Journal of Psychiatry*, U.S. National Library of Medicine, Dec. 2009, http://www.ncbi.nlm.nih.gov/pmc/articles/PMC2802370/.
32. McFadden, Cynthia. "Power of Prayer: What Happens to Your Brain When You Pray?" *NBC News*, 24 Dec. 2014, http://www.nbcnews.com/news/religion/power-prayer-what-happens-your-brain-when-you-pray-n273956.

Chapter 17: Hung on a Tree

33. Alasko, Carl. "How Does Denial Actually Work?" *Psychology Today*, 23 Apr. 2012, http://www.psychologytoday.com/us/blog/beyond-blame/201204/how-does-denial-actually-work.
34. "Denial." *Psychology Today*, http://www.psychologytoday.com/us/basics/denial.
35. Ray, M. (2020). *Pontius Pilate*. Britannica. www.britannica.com/biography/Pontius-Pilate
36. "Herod Antipas." *Encyclopædia Britannica*, 5 Jan. 2023, http://www.britannica.com/biography/Herod-Antipas.

Chapter 18: Grafted In

37. Iannotti, Marie. "What Does Grafting Mean When It Comes to Plants?" *The Spruce*, 25 Aug. 2022, http://www.thespruce.com/what-does-grafting-mean-4125565.

Chapter 19: Fruit of the Spirit

38. "Love." *Merriam-Webster,* https://www.merriam-webster.com/dictionary/love.
39. Baumeister, Roy F., and John Tierney. *Willpower: Rediscovering the Greatest Human Strength.* Penguin Books, 2012.

Chapter 20: The Tree of Life

40. LeMind, Anna. "Top 10 Most Common Human Fears and Phobias." *Learning Mind,* 25 May 2014, https://www.learning-mind.com/top-10-most-common-human-fears-and-phobias/.
41. Dibble, Lauren. "20 Medicinal Trees You Can Forage Medicine From." *Hillsborough Homesteading*, 22 Dec. 2022, https://hillsborough-homesteading.com/medicinal-trees-forage-medicine/.
42. Covey, Stephen R. *7 Habits of Highly Effective People*. Simon and Schuster, 2013.

About the Author

Kristin Arbuckle is an author, designer, photographer, and homeschooling mama of three amazing girls and one independent young man. Kristin graduated from the Bear Valley Bible Institute's Women's Program. She and her husband Andrew have served as domestic missionaries in Hawaii, at a small church plant in Omaha, and have been blessed to sit at the feet of many amazing teachers. Kristin enjoys art of all kinds, good food, reading, and spending time in God's beautiful world!

CPSIA information can be obtained
at www.ICGtesting.com
Printed in the USA
LVHW072314060523
746316LV00005B/11